A Second Opinion....

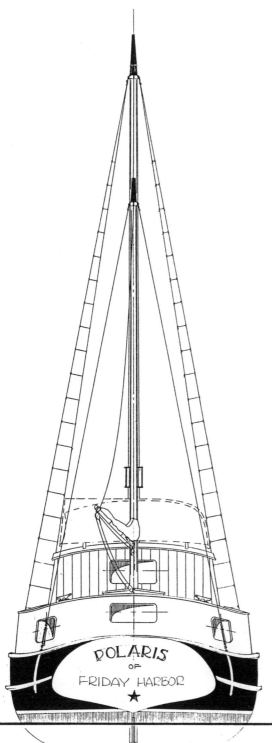

ABOUT THE AUTHOR:

Jay Benford was taken sailing before he could walk, by parents unconcerned about the impressions being made on the youth. He was several years old before he determined that this might not have been perfectly normal procedure on the part of his parents. By then, of course, it was too late for he had become hooked on cruising. His school teachers' pointed remarks about the lack of variety on his book reports (always nautical books) seem to have been of no concern to him. His two years at the University of Michigan led to a much better knowledge of the location of the nautical sections of the libraries than the locations of his classrooms....

He says the best parts of his education were his apprenticeship with John Atkin and the subsequent jobs with a number of boatbuilding firms. After seven years of working for others, he opened his own yacht design office full time in the spring of 1969. Shortly thereafter he got a series of instructive lessons from his accountant in the use of red ink....

He has lived aboard for well over a decade, living on both sail and power boats, and brings this experience to all his design work. His recent design work varies from small craft to freighter yachts to a 40 meter (131') ketch. When not off cruising, he can be found in his St. Michaels, Maryland, office working on one of his dozen or so current design projects.

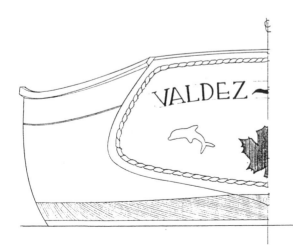

BY THE SAME AUTHOR:

CRUISING BOATS, SAIL & POWER, 4 editions in 1968, 1969, 1970 & 1971. Design catalog and article reprints. OP*

PRACTICAL FERRO-CEMENT BOATBUILDING, with Herman Husen, 3 editions in 1970, 1971 & 1972. Best-selling construction handbook, a how-to on ferro-cement. OP*

DESIGNS & SERVICES, 7 editions, 1971, 1972, 1987, 1988, 1990, 1993 & 1996. Catalog of plans & services of our firm.

BOATBUILDING & DESIGN FORUM, 1973. A monthly newsletter with more information on ferro-cement boatbuilding & other boatbuilding information. OP*

THE BENFORD 30, 3 editions in 1975, 1976 & 1977. An exposition on the virtues of this design and general philosophy on choosing a cruising boat. OP*

CRUISING DESIGNS, 4 editions in 1975, 1976, 1993 & 1996. A catalog of plans and services and information about boats and equipment.

DESIGN DEVELOPMENT OF A 40METER SAILING YACHT, 1981. A technical paper presented to the Society of Naval Architects & Marine Engineers, at the fifth Chesapeake Sailing Yacht Symposium, and in the bound transactions of that meeting.

CRUISING YACHTS, 1983. A hard cover book with a selection of Benford designs covered in detail, including several complete sets of plans, a lot of information about the boats and how they came to be. Eight pages of color photos. OP*

THE FLORIDA BAY COASTERS, A FAMILY OF SMALL SHIPS, 1988. A book of study plans of these Benford designed freighter yachts. OP*

SMALL CRAFT PLANS, 2 printings in 1990 and 1991. A book with fifteen sets of full plans for 7'-3" to 18'-0" dinghies and tenders.

SMALL SHIPS, 4 editions, 1990, 1992 & 1995. A book of study plans for Benford designs for tugs, freighters (like the Florida Bay Coasters), ferries, excursion boats, trawler yachts, houseboats & fishing vessels. Ten pages of color photos.

POCKET CRUISERS & TABLOID YACHTS, Volume 1, 1992. A book with 6 complete sets of plans (11 boats including the different versions) for boats from 14' to 25', including 14' & 20' Tug Yachts, 17' & 25' Fantail Steam Launches, a 14' Sloop, a 20' Catboat, and 20' Supply Boat & Cruiser.

* OP = Out of print

Cruising Designs

A Catalog Of Plans For Cruising Boats, Sail & Power
From The Boards Of The

Benford Design Group

Mail: P. O. Box 447
Office: 605 Talbot Street
St. Michaels, MD 21663

Voice: 410-745-3235
Fax: 410-745-9743

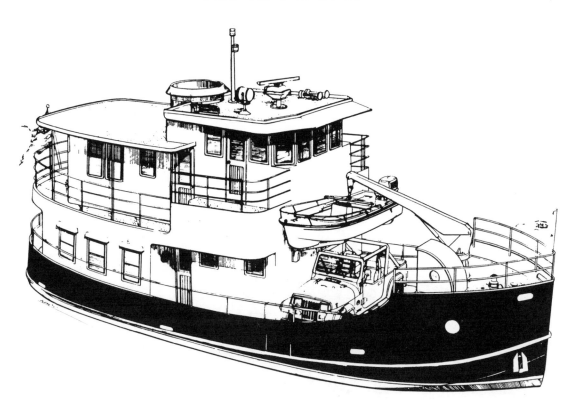

Tiller Publishing

P. O. Box 447
605 Talbot Street
St. Michaels, MD 21663

Voice: 410-745-3750
Fax: 410-745-9743

Dedication:

To our design clients, without whom we wouldn't have had the opportunities to design most of these Cruising Designs. Their input and pushing us to explore new solutions have made life interesting and entertaining for the last three decades.

Layout and design by Tiller Publishing. Photos supplied by the author, except as noted. Cover illustrations by Steve Davis, with the front cover courtesy of **Sail** magazine.

INTRODUCTION

CHANGES IN THE 4TH EDITION

The last sixteen pages represent a portion of the new work we've done since the 3rd edition was printed. More of our new design work on powerboats can be found in our **SMALL SHIPS, THIRD EDITION** book. If your interest is in a powerboat, this is the volume that I'd recommend to you.

DESIGNS & SERVICES

If your copy of **CRUISING DESIGNS** arrived without a copy of our price list, please contact us and we'll get one right back to you. It has a lot of information in it along with the prices for all the plans currently available.

CUSTOM DESIGNS & CONTRACT FORM

Also included is our information about custom designs and our custom design contract. This is done so that those who are considering hiring a naval architect or yacht designer will know what to expect and how we do business.

THE INDEX IS UP FRONT....

We've combined the Index and Table Of Contents on the following two pages to try to make it easier to track down which ever size, type or specific boat is of interest.

THE BENFORD DESIGN GROUP

The Benford Design Group is a loosely knit group of highly skilled people. Each has extended and varied skills and experiences that lend depth and breadth to our design work, and how we can go about problem solving in making existing boats better. We do consulting work on a variety of projects including designs by others and existing boats that need modification. Our structural design experience extends to some of the largest cold-molded and composite boats ever built. We've worked with several of the various classification societies and the U. S. Coast Guard in providing designs and meeting their requirements.

THE ADULT TOY BUSINESS

There is an aspect to our business that could be thought of as being in the adult toy business. It is certainly fun for us and it seems that our clients have a good time too. However, our approach to designing is very serious, for we pride ourselves on being innovative and practical in creating boats that are easy to use and to build. Our structures are done with a weather eye to longevity and hard service, and so should hold up well for a long time in normal service.

We also realize that you want to complete each cruise you begin....

Our favorite occupation, and the one that fills most of our time, is the creation of custom designs for yachts and commercial vessels. Each design is drawn up to fill the special needs of an individual client. Thus, our plans are for those who want something more than that which is available in stock boats. The arrangements and layouts are designed for maximum usage and livability for often smaller than normal crews. The profiles are expressions of the individuality of the various owners and are not the sort that will be in style today and out tomorrow. Over the years, as we create more and more ideas to satisfy these individual requirements, we have built up quite a file of stock plans. A number of these are also available as stock production hulls, which can be custom outfitted by the original builder, by your favorite shipyard, or in your own shop.

We hope the illustrations in this book will entice you to delve further into our designs. We're having fun creating them, and find boats to be a grand way of life. The special and individual natures of each of our many clients are capsulized in the selection of vessels shown over the following pages. We'd enjoy being able to include your boat in the future books of our designs and will look forward to helping you get your new boat underway.

The boats shown were selected from the custom designs done over the past three decades and are offered for sale as stock plans. Custom designing is available for special projects and can be quoted on receipt of details of what is desired. Designs for commercial boats can also be provided on the same basis. Modifications of stock plans — different arrangement, engine, building materials and so on — can be made to provide a custom boat with savings in the initial design fee.

Perhaps one of these vessels will be the spark to fire your ideas of the sort of boat you really want, or will suggest to you an idea for your new boat. Let us know what you want and we'll get some figures back to you on what we can put together and the scheduling for getting it out.

Jay R. Benford
Yacht *Odyssea*
St. Michaels, MD
June 1996

INDEX & TABLE OF CONTENTS

BY SIZE (LENGTH/TYPE):

ALPHABETICAL ORDER:

| 17' Catboat Puffin | 17' Cruising Cat Liberty | 17' Cruising Sloop | 17' Cruising Yawl | 17' Gaff Sloop | 17' Sloop | 17' Cutter |

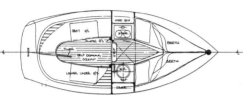

17' Catboat Puffin

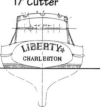

Puffin & Liberty
17' Catboat & Cruising Cat
Design number 67
1970

This handsome tabloid cruiser accommodates two, either in a V-berth/double or singles. She has a head, stove, and plenty of storage space. The sink, counter, lounging seat and hanging locker for oilskins are additions in Cruising Cat version, which has a shorter cockpit and an optional deeper keel with room for an inboard engine. Inboard or outboard power of 5 to 10 horsepower is all that is needed. She has a deep, self-draining cockpit, she performs well in light airs and is able to carry full sail in 20 knots of wind. A safe, sane investment — an ideal first boat for the amateur builder. The alternate rigs, taken from the 18' Canoe Yawl and 20' Gaff Sloop, can be used on the basic 17' Catboat hull. Optional interior details can be expanded by way of joinery details and sections on a custom basis to order. An alternative Marconi sloop rig is also available, as are gaff cutter and topsail sloop rigs.

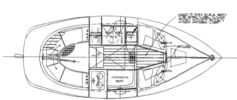

17' Cruising Cat Liberty

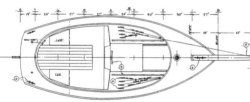

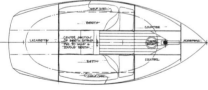

17' Gaff Sloop

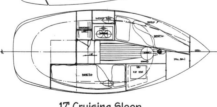

17' Cruising Sloop

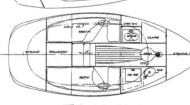

17' Cruising Yawl

Particulars:		17'	19'	26'-3"
Length overall		17'-0"	19' 0"	26'-3"
Length designed waterline		15'-1½"	16'-9"	24'-0"
Beam		7'-0"	7'-0"	9'-6"
Draft		2'-6" or 3'-6"	3'-6" or 2'-6"	4'-6"
Freeboard:	Forward	3'-4"	3'-4"	4'-3¼"
	Least	1'-11"	1'-11"	2'-7 3/8"
	Aft	2'-2"	2'-2"	3'-0"
Displacement, cruising trim. lbs.		2,950 or 3,600	3,025 or 4,120	11,000
Displacement-length ratio		381 or 464	287 or 391	355
Ballast		850 or 1,200	900 or 1,200	3,300
Ballast ratio		29% or 41%	29%	30%
Sail area, square feet		200 to 300	254 to 342	560
Sail area-displacement ratio		13.62 to 23.34	15.81 to 21.29	18.12
Prismatic coefficient		.53	.544 or .539	.562
Pounds per inch immersion		356	390	736
Entrance half-angle		26°	22°	21°
Water tankage, gallons		20	13	40
Fuel tankage, gallons		10	13	20
Headroom		4'-4" to 4'-10"	4'-4" to 4'-10"	6'-2"

19' Cruising Sloop

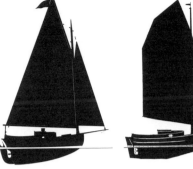

19' Cruising Cat Scrimshaw

19' Lug Sloop

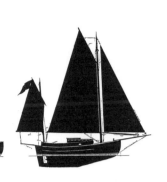

19' Cruising Yawl

26'-3" Cruising Cutter

Scrimshaw
19' Cruising Cat or Sloop
Design number 177
1978

This 19-footer is a longer version of our very popular and successful 17' **Puffin** and **Liberty** versions. Like them there is both a deep and an alternate shallow keel version available, along with a sloop rig, lug sloop rig or yawl rig options.

"There's some truth to the saying that smaller boats are harder to design well than larger ones. There is always the temptation to try drawing in more accommodations than the hull can reasonably be expected to hold. Yet, if some modicum of comfort is missing, prospective buyers will be reluctant to plunk down their hard-earned cash. Full-length berths and provisions for a head and galley space are usually deemed minimum requirements.

"The **Scrimshaw 19** succeeds admirably in meeting this design challenge, and should exceed many persons' expectations for good looks. Those committed to pocket cruisers sometimes feel neglected because of the relatively small number of boats to choose from, especially under 20 feet. Jay Benford is one designer who seems to enjoy working for the small guy as well as for the client whose tastes and pocketbook demand the "ultimate maxi."

"Jay says that when Lin and Larry Pardey stopped in to visit one day, he showed them the rough draft of the lines for the **Scrimshaw 19**. They both agreed her sections looked much like **Seraffyn**'s. She has a long keel and outboard rudder, so she should have the feel of a larger boat. This will be especially true considering her designed displacement of 4,120 pounds. Benford cautions readers of his plans that "cruising displacement" means he has included the weight of fuel and water, crew and gear....

"Comfort seems to have been the watchword in designing the **Scrimshaw 19**, and this is clearly evident in he cockpit. The coamings are 13 to 17 inches high and are sloped outboard to prevent sore backs. The footwell width is calculated to be just right for bracing a foot from the other side. A hatch in the cockpit floor provides ready access to the small inboard diesel engine."

Cruising World

19' Lug Sloop

26'-3" Cruising Cutter
Design number 187
1979

A modern evolution of the English Channel cutters, like them the 26'-3" Cruising Cutter is fast, stiff and weatherly. Her stability curve shows that she has a very long range of positive stability with minimal negative area — all indicative of a stiff and powerful boat with the power to carry sail in a blow and be able to sail her way out of trouble. She has standing headroom in a practical and roomy layout, whether living aboard or voyaging.

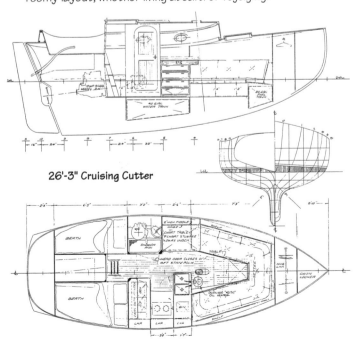

26'-3" Cruising Cutter

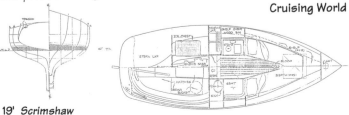

19' Scrimshaw

23' Canoe Yawl

23' Gaff Sloop

18' Catboat

18' Gaff Sloop

18' Canoe Yawl

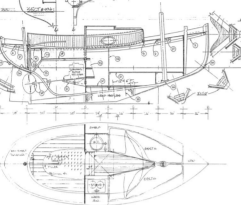

18' Canoe Yawl

18' & 23' Canoe Yawls
Designs Number 28 & 112
1969 & 1973

These little yawls are bound to turn heads in any harbor into which they venture. The split rig doubles the pleasure of sailing her! And, the mizzen will help hold her steadily head to wind in an anchorage and make her easier to balance for self-steering.

The 18 is laid out to sleep two in V-berths which can also be converted into a large double if the crew desires a more cozy arrangement. A head, stove, inboard power, long straight ballast keel, self-draining cockpit and split rig make this a true cruising vessel — pocket sized!

The 18-footer is available with the 17' Catboat's or 20' Gaff Sloop's rigs as options. Also, the 22' Knockabout's rig could be used on her. There is also a small fish hold version, which was used on **Iota**, one of the first 18-footers built. She sailed from Seattle to Alaska and back, serving as home for her crew for over a year.

The attractive 23' big sister to the 18' Canoe Yawl should prove of appeal to canoe-stern enthusiasts. With 6'-2" headroom in her cabin, she's comfortable for longer voyages, and affords a surprising amount of accommodations in just 23 feet of length. A large single (or small double) berth to port and single berth to starboard foot beneath the cockpit, with their forward ends making comfortable lounging seats next to the ice box and sink to starboard and counter & wood range to port. Forward there are two V-berths with bookshelves outboard and head between, or a double berth to one side. A large stowage area in the lazarette is representative of the accommodating amount of stowage space in the rest of the vessel. This vessel has been optionally gaff cutter rigged, using the gaff cutter Sail Plan from the 25' Gaff Sloop or Marconi Cutter rigged using the rig from the 27' Cutter.

18' Iota

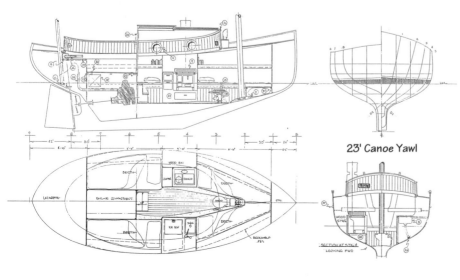

23' Canoe Yawl

Particulars:		28	112
Length overall		18'-0"	23'-0"
Length designed waterline		16'-0"	21'-0"
Beam		7'-0"	8'-9"
Draft		3'-0"	4'-0"
Freeboard:	Forward	3'-6"	3'-3"
	Least	2'-0½"	2'-2½"
	Aft	2'-6"	2'-9¼"
Displacement, cruising trim		4,200 lbs.	8,940 lbs.
Displacement-length ratio		458	431
Ballast		1,500 lbs.	2,400 lbs.
Ballast ratio		36%	27%
Sail area		233 sq. ft.	450 sq. ft.
Sail area-displacement ratio		14.32	16.72
Pounds per inch immersion		382	592
Entrance half-angle		27°	23°
Water tankage		Gals.	15 Gals.
Fuel tankage		Gals.	15 Gals.
Headroom		4'-9" to 5'-0"	6'-2"

22' Sloop

22' Knockabout

22' Lug Sloop

22' Pilothouse Sloop

22' Knockabout
Cascade Classic 22
Design number 111
1973 & 1975

From top to bottom, the versions at right are the 22' Sloop with double berth forward, the 22' Knockabout with settees that convert to double berth aft, the optional raised-flush-deck, the longer house version of the 22' Sloop with quarter-berths, and the 22' Pilothouse Version.

This handsome pocket cruiser reflects simplicity of line, rig and construction. Going by the traditional definition of a "knockabout", she is indeed a sailing vessel of simple sloop rig having just a jib and mainsail, and no bowsprit. For the coast-wise voyager, there is a good deal of stowage room below decks. A unique feature is the potential for a king size bed! (Port and starboard settee/berths extend at the same height as the step from the cockpit underneath the cockpit seats and sole on several versions.) The 22' Knockabout's simple rig only has 3 stays.

The version with the longer waterline is the one designed for 'glass production. The interiors and rigs are pretty much interchangeable. Molded 'glass hulls are available as shells or outfitted as completely as you'd like. Call or write us for more particulars on these finely built boats!

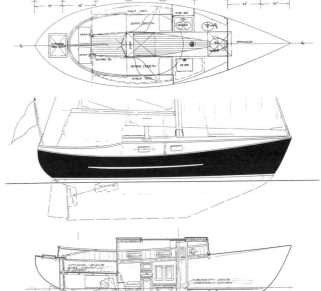

Particulars:

Length overall		22'-0"
Length designed waterline		17'-0"/18'-0"
Beam		7'-0"
Draft		4'-0"/3'-9"
Freeboard:	Forward	3'-6"/3'-6½"
	Least	2'-0½"/2'-1 3/8"
	Aft	2'-8½"/2'-9¼"
Displacement, cruising trim		4,705/4,000 lbs.
Displacement-length ratio		428/306
Ballast		1,600/1,400 lbs.
Ballast ratio		34/35%
Sail area: Knockabout		254 sq. ft.
Masthead rig		215-315 sq. ft.
Sail area-displacement ratio:		
Knockabout		14.47 or 16.13
Masthead rig		12.25 to 17.95/
		13.65 to 20.00
Prismatic coefficient		.512/.522
Pounds per inch immersion		393/402
Entrance half-angle		22½°/21°
Water tankage		/16 Gals.
Fuel tankage		/12 Gals.
Headroom		5'-0"/5'-1"

Rich Green's 22-Footer

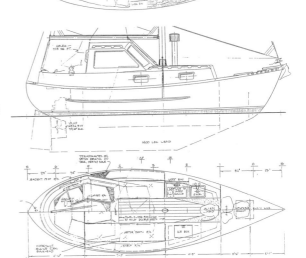

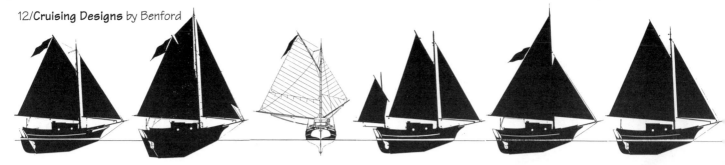

20' Gaff Sloop Ragnar   20' Topsail Sloop   20' Sloop Stern View   20' Yawl Version   20' Marconi Sloop   20' Tall Sloop Rig

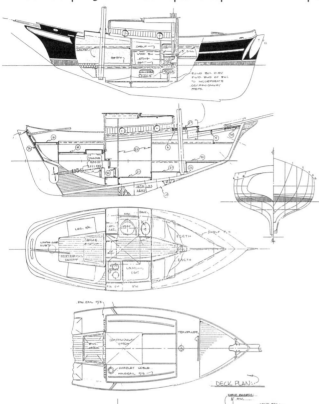

20' Gaff Sloop Ragnar (Roy Montgomery photo)

20'-26' Friendship Sloops

Designs Number 68, 160, 91 & 138
1971, 1977, 1972 & 1976

20: The first one built to this design was the **Ragnar**, which was our company yacht for a while. We had a great time cruising and daysailing her — and her handsome appearance drew crowds, making it easy for us to meet people wherever we sailed. She's a handsome and handy pocket cruiser for two and can daysail up to six. Her features include a long, straight, ballast keel, cutaway forefoot for easy maneuvering, self-draining cockpit, spacious cockpit and interior, inboard diesel power, with an option for an outboard in a well. She's suitable for coastwise cruising, and a reasonable project for the skilled amateur builder.

We've adapted the rigs from some of our other tabloid yachts for use on **Ragnar** and these are shown in the silhouettes above.

21: This is a variation on the 20-footer, with a radically modified underbody, for better performance in lighter airs and the prospect of improved tacking ability. (Our 20-footer would do 80 degrees tack-to-tack, though, so is no slouch....) Built carefully, she can be quite a bit lighter and still have the classic Friendship Sloop appearance.

25: An enlarged version of the 20' Gaff Sloop, this 25-footer extends the flair of her little sister. Her main cabin has 6'-2" headroom and 6'-6" berths each side. Hinged upper berths could be fitted, to function as backrests during daytime, or the starboard berth could be made to extend to a double. The head is forward in its own compartment, and a 10 h.p. inboard diesel engine, although an outboard could alternately be fitted, if preferred. With the same hull and interior arrangement as the 25' Gaff Sloop, the Marconi Cutter offers a slightly different sail type for those who feel more at home on a Marconi rig.

26: A slightly longer version of the 25, with a fin keel underbody, this one has an arrangement that will be very comfortable for a couple to vacation or live aboard. The sleeping area is forward, out of the living and socializing in the saloon. There is an enclosed head, a one-fold chart table, good sized galley, guest/sea berth, settee and drop-leaf table with good room for two couples.

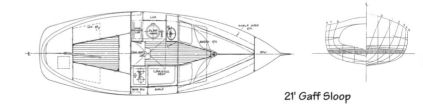

21' Gaff Sloop

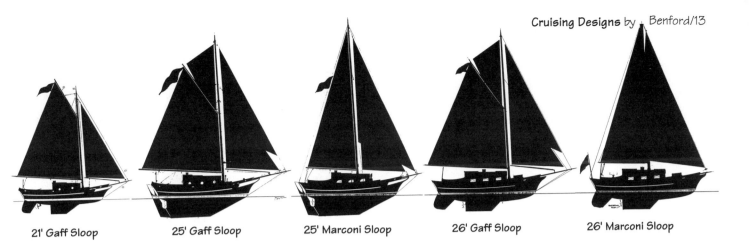

21' Gaff Sloop   25' Gaff Sloop   25' Marconi Sloop   26' Gaff Sloop   26' Marconi Sloop

26' Marconi Sloop
by Tony Cox

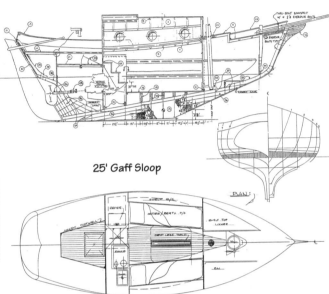

25' Gaff Sloop

26' Gaff Sloop

Particulars:		68	160	91	138
Length Overall		20'-0"	21'-6"	25'-0"	26'-6"
Length Designed Waterline		16'-0"	17'-0"	20'-0"	21'-6"
Beam		7'-0"	7'-1"	8'-9"	9'-0"
Draft		3'-0"/4'-0"	3'-0"	3'-9"/4'-6"	3'-9"
Freeboard:	Forward	3'-7"	3'-4¼"	3'-10"	4'-4"
	Least	1'-10½"	1'-10¾"	2'-4"	2'-4"
	Aft	2'-4"	3'-0"	2'-11"	3'-3"
Displacement, Cruising Trim, Lbs.		3,600/4,200	3,000	7,000/7,600	6,600
Displacement-Length Ratio		392/458	273	391/424	296
Ballast, Pounds		1450	900	2,000	2,400
Ballast Ratio,		35/40	30	26/29	36
Sail Area, Square Feet		210	260	350	350
Tops'l. Rig W/Genoa, Sq. Ft.		300	300	515	515
Sail Area-Displacement Ratio		12.91/14.30	20.00	15.30/14.49	15.92
Topsail Rig W/Genoa		18.44/20.43	23.08	22.52/21.32	23.42
Prismatic Coefficient		.51	.51	.51	.56
Pounds Per Inch Immersion		357	374	558	605
Water/Fuel Tankage, Gals.		15/12		14/20	50/20
Headroom		5'-0"	4'-4"	6'-2"	6'-0"

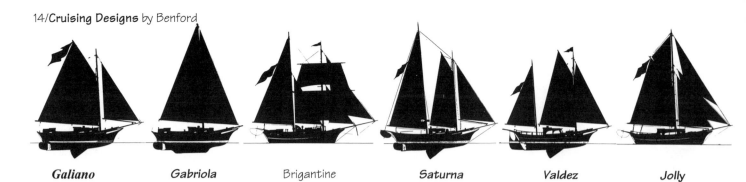

Galiano   *Gabriola*   Brigantine   *Saturna*   *Valdez*   *Jolly*

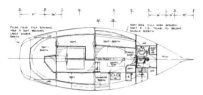

Galiano ⇧

Bakea sistership ⇧   *Belle Amie* sistership ⇩

The Benford 30 Series
Designs Number 52, 70, 101 & 173
1969, 1971, 1975, & 1978

The wide range of variations shown in the silhouettes on these two pages is a good indication of how popular these 30-footers are. Starting with the centerboarders above, with an optional outside ballast keel, we progressed to the wineglass keel version below. Then, with the advent of the fiberglass versions, we had another keel version shown at top on the next page. The powerboat versions, below right, can be done with either the shoal or the deep keel, either from the mold or as one-offs.

The heritage of this classic cruising vessel stems from the Friendship Sloop type, with a bit of catboat influence. We have raised her freeboard to increase living accommodations, cut away her forefoot to quicken maneuvering, and slightly modified the volume distribution of her hull to minimize drag and increase speed. We have further modified her keel sections for solid lead and concrete ballast and shaped the keel for maximum performance.

There is a wide selection of rigs and interiors available on this basic hull, from Great Cabin Cutter to Sloop, Schooner, Ketch, Brigantine, Motorsailer, Trawler Yacht, or Motor Launch. Fiberglass hulls for her

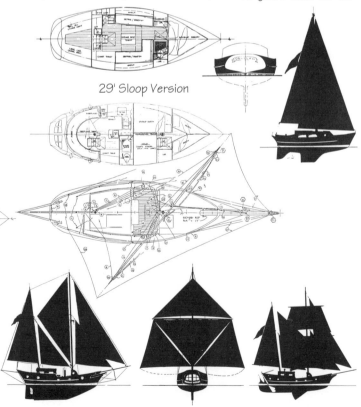

29' Sloop Version

Belle Amie and alternate interior

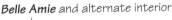

Belle Amie Schooner and alternate Marconi Ketch and Cutter rigs   31' Square Topsail Ketch Version, With Keel Or Centerboard

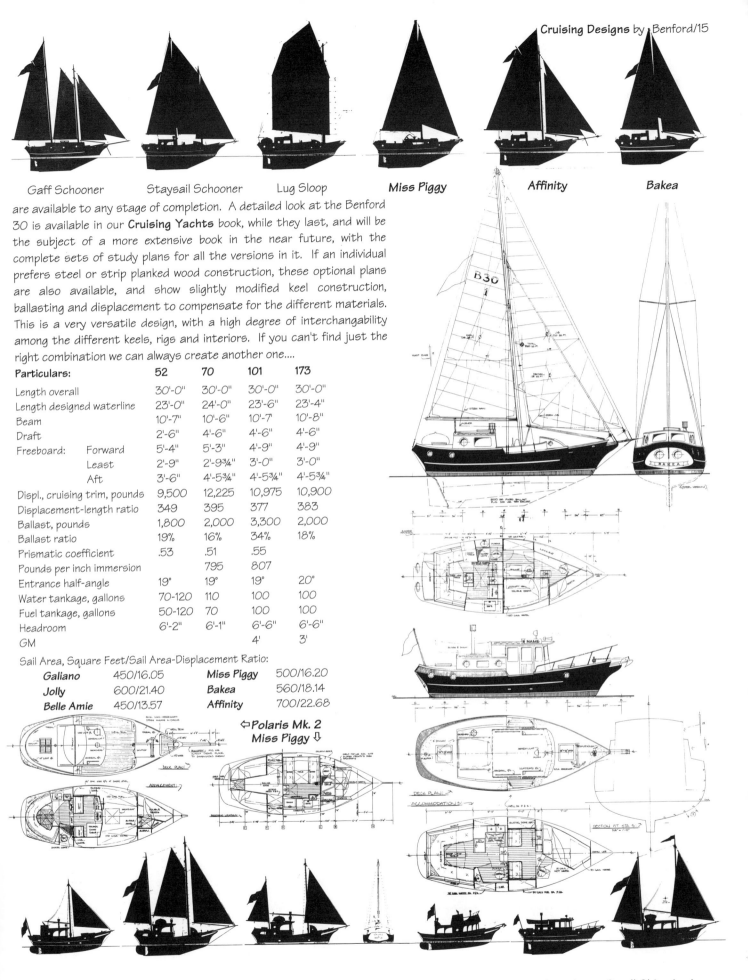

Gaff Schooner   Staysail Schooner   Lug Sloop   **Miss Piggy**   *Affinity*   *Bakea*

are available to any stage of completion. A detailed look at the Benford 30 is available in our **Cruising Yachts** book, while they last, and will be the subject of a more extensive book in the near future, with the complete sets of study plans for all the versions in it. If an individual prefers steel or strip planked wood construction, these optional plans are also available, and show slightly modified keel construction, ballasting and displacement to compensate for the different materials. This is a very versatile design, with a high degree of interchangability among the different keels, rigs and interiors. If you can't find just the right combination we can always create another one....

Particulars:		52	70	101	173
Length overall		30'-0"	30'-0"	30'-0"	30'-0"
Length designed waterline		23'-0"	24'-0"	23'-6"	23'-4"
Beam		10'-7"	10'-6"	10'-7"	10'-8"
Draft		2'-6"	4'-6"	4'-6"	4'-6"
Freeboard:	Forward	5'-4"	5'-3"	4'-9"	4'-9"
	Least	2'-9"	2'-9¾"	3'-0"	3'-0"
	Aft	3'-6"	4'-5¾"	4'-5¾"	4'-5¾"
Displ., cruising trim, pounds		9,500	12,225	10,975	10,900
Displacement-length ratio		349	395	377	383
Ballast, pounds		1,800	2,000	3,300	2,000
Ballast ratio		19%	16%	34%	18%
Prismatic coefficient		.53	.51	.55	
Pounds per inch immersion			795	807	
Entrance half-angle		19°	19°	19°	20°
Water tankage, gallons		70-120	110	100	100
Fuel tankage, gallons		50-120	70	100	100
Headroom		6'-2"	6'-1"	6'-6"	6'-6"
GM				4'	3'

Sail Area, Square Feet/Sail Area-Displacement Ratio:

Galiano	450/16.05	*Miss Piggy*	500/16.20
Jolly	600/21.40	*Bakea*	560/18.14
Belle Amie	450/13.57	*Affinity*	700/22.68

⇐ *Polaris Mk. 2*
Miss Piggy ⇩

Polaris Mk. 1, 3, 2, Orion, B30 Trawler and Motorsailer.   All these powerboat versions are shown in our **Small Ships** book.

34'-6" Schooner   34'-6" Cutter   38' Ketch

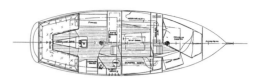

34'-6" Schooner

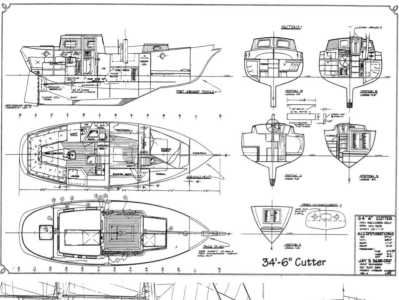

34'-6" Cutter

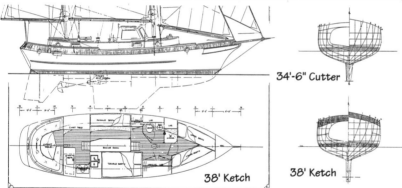

34'-6" Cutter

38' Ketch

38' Ketch

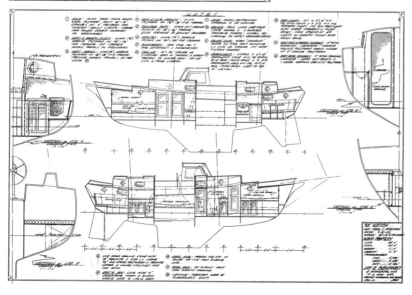

Benford 34½ & 38

Designs Number 188 & 126
1979 & 1977

These are larger sisters to the popular Benford 30 series. The 34½ has two variations on the great cabin layout. The schooner layout (above) has a piano and the cutter (at left) has inside steering like **Bakea**.

We took all the lessons we'd learned about how well the B30 worked and applied them to the creation of the 34½. The result is a boat with more storage spaces and more elbow room. The finer entry to the hull form will make for a slightly closer-winded boat and the extra length will make for a bit more speed.

The 38 was originally started as a long keel (5' draft) version of **Bakea** with a similar great cabin layout. These variations could be done yet on the final version of the design, which is shown below left.

The pilothouse on the 38 is really a hard dodger, which can be closed in with canvas or left open in good weather. I've been assured that the liking, or at least acceptance, of a dodger or deckhouse is the sign of a sensible man with some real experience in cruising. Like many of our designs, this one will be not only a voyager but a home afloat for her owner. Thus her layout is a balance between comfort in port and at sea. Her sleeping accommodations are amidships and forward, though the great cabin settee might also be made into berths.

Particulars:		188	126
Length overall		34'-6"	38'-0"
Length designed waterline		28'-0"	30'-6"
Beam		11'-0"	11'-0"
Draft		5'-0"	5'-9"
Freeboard:	Forward	5'-3 3/8"	5'-9¾"
	Least	3'-6"	3'-10¾"
	Aft	4'-9"	5'-3¼"
Displacement, cruising trim		16,064 lbs.	16,675 lbs.
Displacement-length ratio		327	263
Ballast		5,000 lbs.	6,200 lbs.
Ballast ratio		31%	37%
Sail area:			850 sq. ft.
Schooner/Cutter		700/705 sq. ft.	
Sail area-displacement ratio:			20.8
Schooner/Cutter		17.59/17.72	
Prismatic coefficient		.56	.57
Pounds per inch immersion		1,026	1,118
Entrance half-angle		23¼°	21°
Water tankage		Gals.	110 Gals.
Fuel tankage		Gals.	75 Gals.
Headroom		4'-9" to 6'-6"	5'-6" to 6'-8"

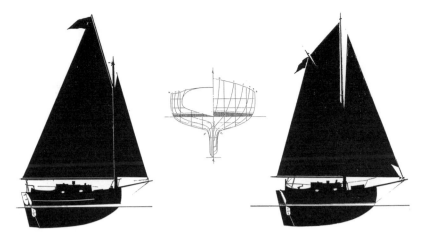

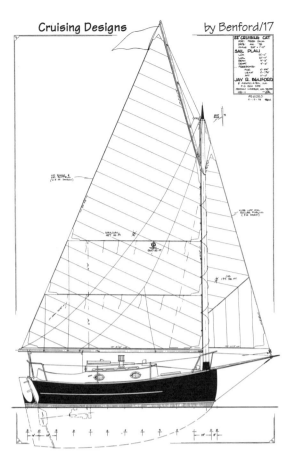

Particulars:

Length overall		22'-0"	Sail area: Cutter/Catboat		603/560 sq. ft.
Length designed waterline		20'-0"	Sail area-displacement ratio:		22.64/21.02
Beam		9'-8"	Wetted Surface (W.S.)		211 sq. ft.
Draft		4'-6"	Sail Area/W.S. Ratio		2.86/2.65
Freeboard:	Forward	4'-3¼"	Prismatic coefficient		.573
	Least	2'-7 3/8"	Pounds per inch immersion		633
	Aft	3'-0"	Entrance half-angle		28°
Displacement, cruising trim		8,800 lbs.	Water tankage		55 Gals.
Displacement-length ratio		491	Fuel tankage		27 Gals.
Ballast		2,200 lbs.	Headroom		6'-2"
Ballast ratio		25%	GM		3'

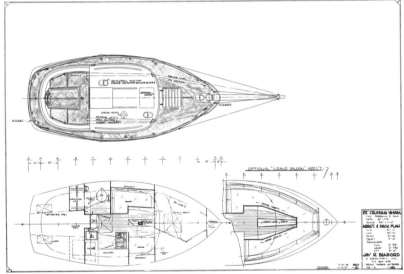

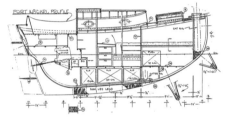

22' Cruising Catboat or Cutter

Design number 128
1975 & 1988

An expanded version of our popular 17' Cruising Catboat, this larger sister has almost twice the room in her proportionately larger hull. She's the answer for those who are in love with the 17' Catboat, but who'd like something "just a little bigger". She has 6'-2" standing headroom and the practicality of the traditional catboat hull about her.

The catboat and topsail cutter rigs give the boat some interesting options. The topsail cutter is the designer's favorite, with the variety of sails making her versatile and easily handled in a variety of conditions with a high fun quotient.

Her heavy displacement gives a great comfort to being aboard, and her hull form with the ballast on the keel give her great stability for carrying sail in a strong breeze. She has very high sail area to wetted surface and displacement ratios to assure good sailing performance in light airs too.

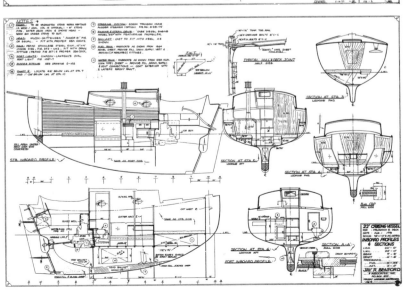

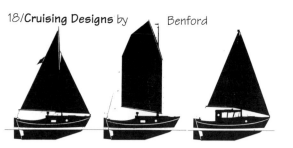

23' Sourdough

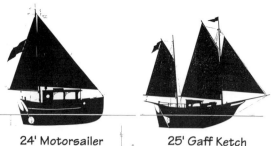

24' Motorsailer   25' Gaff Ketch   26' V-Bottom Ketch

Tabloid Yachts

Designs number 179, 65, 51 & 41
1979, 1970, 1969 & 1967

For those who are not familiar with the terms, a tabloid yacht is a smaller edition of a sailing yacht and a pocket cruiser is a smaller cruising powerboat.

23' Sourdough is a simply built, practical, salty cruiser, capable of doing long cruises with one or two aboard. There are several versions, all of which can work well as motorsailers. The pilothouse version has 6½' headroom.

24' This stout cruising vessel was designed for enjoying the inside passage to Alaska and the fjords of B.C., where neither speed nor ability to windward is a major concern. The deckhouse measures ten feet square and offers unmatched livability for three — complete with separate shower and a galley to rival many apartment kitchens. A cruising speed of about 5 knots is provided by a small diesel of about 20 continuous horsepower.

25' She has a simple, uncrowded layout for two, a v-bottom, with straight frames (except for the slight curved tumblehome aft), straightforward construction. 2,000 pounds lead ballast keel.

26' Comfortably laid out for three, she is intended for coastwise cruising. She has a lot of simple detailing, like her transom stern, outboard rudder. A small inboard could be fitted. There are two rigs, for light and heavy wind areas.

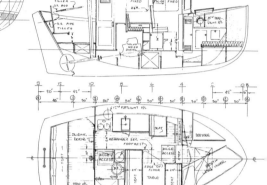

24' Motorsailer

25' Gaff Ketch built by artist Harold Balazs

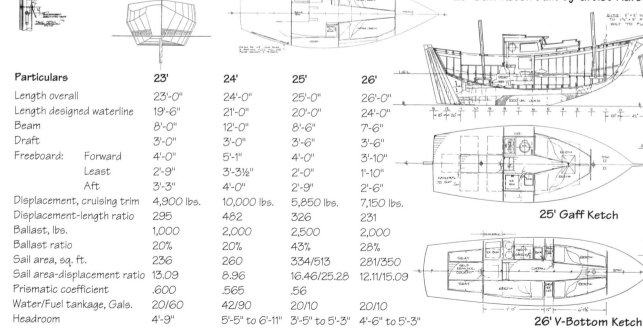

23' Sourdough

25' Gaff Ketch

26' V-Bottom Ketch

Particulars		23'	24'	25'	26'
Length overall		23'-0"	24'-0"	25'-0"	26'-0"
Length designed waterline		19'-6"	21'-0"	20'-0"	24'-0"
Beam		8'-0"	12'-0"	8'-6"	7'-6"
Draft		3'-0"	3'-0"	3'-6"	3'-6"
Freeboard:	Forward	4'-0"	5'-1"	4'-0"	3'-10"
	Least	2'-9"	3'-3½"	2'-0"	1'-10"
	Aft	3'-3"	4'-0"	2'-9"	2'-6"
Displacement, cruising trim		4,900 lbs.	10,000 lbs.	5,850 lbs.	7,150 lbs.
Displacement-length ratio		295	482	326	231
Ballast, lbs.		1,000	2,000	2,500	2,000
Ballast ratio		20%	20%	43%	28%
Sail area, sq. ft.		236	260	334/513	281/350
Sail area-displacement ratio		13.09	8.96	16.46/25.28	12.11/15.09
Prismatic coefficient		.600	.565	.56	
Water/Fuel tankage, Gals.		20/60	42/90	20/10	20/10
Headroom		4'-9"	5'-5" to 6'-11"	3'-5" to 5'-3"	4'-6" to 5'-3"

19' & 22' Gunkholers

Designs Number 19 & 15
1969 & 1965

Large sailing skiffs, these simple cruising vessels are intended for plywood construction, with carvel planking as an option on the 22. The 22 offers five rig options with sail areas ranging from 199 to 330 square feet. She sleeps two or three. The keel version may be fitted with a small inboard. An outboard of about five to ten horsepower will also provide adequate and inexpensive power.

The sturdy little flat bottom 19-foot centerboard catboat, with her shallow draft is ideal for gunkholing where shoals are a concern in one's cruising grounds. With two berths that make into a double, two lounging seats (one over the head) with good sitting headroom, sink, stove and hanging locker, her accommodations are generous for her 19 feet of length. Her catboat rig and plywood construction spell simplicity and practicality. Paul Miller's *Catspaw* was the first of this series and has proven to be very practical and salty little cruiser. With the very shallow draft, there's hardly any need for a dinghy, for the boat can be beached.

P.S. The common definition of a "gunkhole" is a very shallow body of water, usually with a soft and sticky bottom. Thus the name for these shallow draft cruisers.

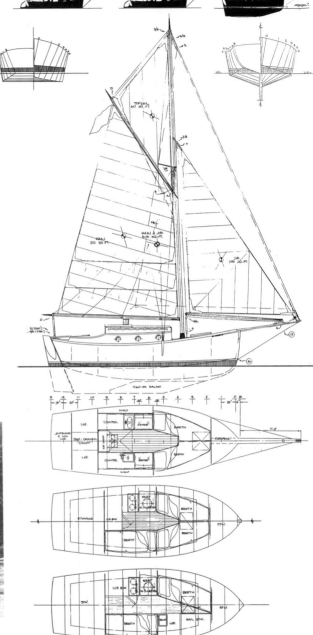

19' *Catspaw* and *Sylvester* built by Paul Miller.

19' Catspaw (below) & 22' Variations (above)

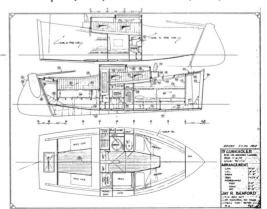

Particulars:	19'	22'	22'V
Length overall	19'-6"	22'-0"	22'-0"
Length designed waterline	18'-0"	20'-0"	20'-0"
Beam	7'-9"	8'-0"	8'-0"
Draft, c.b. up/down	1'-4"/4'-8"	1'-4"/3'-10"	3'-0"
Freeboard: Forward	3'-8"	3'-10"	4'-0"
Least	2'-0"	2'-0"	2'-4"
Aft	2'-7"	2'-6"	3'-0"
Displacement, cruising trim	3,475 lbs.	4,750 lbs.	4,500 lbs.
Displacement-length ratio	266	265	253
Ballast, lbs.	500	900	1,260
Ballast ratio	14%	19%	28%
Sail area, square feet	256	199 to 330	310 to 638
Sail area-displacement ratio	17.85	11.27 to 18.69	18.20 to 37.45
Prismatic coefficient	.613		.547
Headroom	4'-8½"	4'-3" to 5'-1"	5'-1" to 5'-3"

26' Raised Deck Cutter **30' Ketch** **30' Gaff Cutter** **30' Pilothouse Cutter** **32' Ketch Shoestring** **34' Badger**

Sailing Dory Designs
The Most Economical Offshore Cruisers

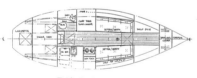

26' Raised Deck Cutter

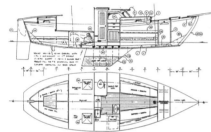

30' Ketch

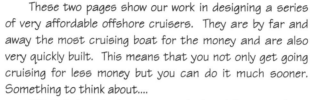

30' Gaff Cutter

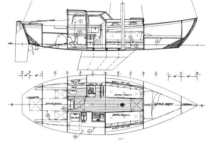

30' Pilothouse Cutter

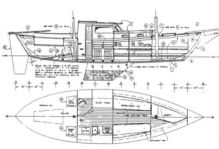

32' Ketch Shoestring

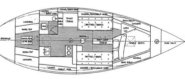

34' Lug Schooner Badger

34' Cutter

These two pages show our work in designing a series of very affordable offshore cruisers. They are by far and away the most cruising boat for the money and are also very quickly built. This means that you not only get going cruising for less money but you can do it much sooner. Something to think about....

26: This twin keel cutter was designed for a couple to do long distance voyaging aboard. She is capable of doing long voyages, but does not have as generous storage space aboard as the larger ones.

30: This simple-to-construct, no-nonsense little 30-footer will show the performance available with these simply built voyagers. Though flat-bottomed in dory fashion, when she's heeled over, she presents a "V" to the water, and will move along at a good clip. She has 2,400 pound lead ballast on her keel, with plywood, hard chine construction over framing of bulkheads and her furniture. She has an enclosed head, a functional galley and a roomy area for dining and lounging.

32: Named **Shoestring** in honor of one of the first ones built, this name perfectly fits the design philosophy. Intended as an inexpensive cruiser for four, she is another ideal project for the amateur builder — or for the

*Caution: The displacement quoted here is for the boat in coastal cruising trim. That is, with the fuel and water tanks filled, the crew on board, as well as the crews' gear and stores in the lockers. This should not be confused with the "shipping weight" often quoted as "displacement" by some manufacturers. This should be taken into account when comparing figures and ratios between this and other designs. Also, loading down for voyaging and living aboard, as with the Hill's **Badger**, will add considerably to these figures, perhaps as much as 50%. Designs like **Badger**, which load down gracefully and still sail well, make a good choice for anyone wanting to go voyaging on a small income.

Sailing Dory Particulars:

Size		26'	30'	32'	34'	36'	37½'
Length Overall		26'-0"	30'-0"	32'-0"	34'-0"	36'-0"	37'-6"
Length Datum Waterline		23'-1"	26'-0"	27'-0"	28'-0"	31'-0"	31'-0"
Beam		9'-9¾"	10'-0"	9'-0"	11'-0"	11'-0"	11'-0"
Draft		3'-0"	4'-0"	4'-0"	4'-6"	4'-6"	4'-6"
Freeboard:	Forward	4'-6"	4'-6"	4'-2"	5'-0"	5'-0¾"	5'-2½"
	Least	4'-4½"	2'-8¾"	2'-6¼"	2'-9"	3'-0¼"	3'-0¼"
	Aft	3'-8½"	3'-3½"	3'-6½"	4'-0"	4'-2¾"	4'-9"
Displacement, Cruising Trim*		8,000	6,700	6,900	10,400	13,425	13,425
Displacement-Length Ratio		290	170	156	211	201	201
Ballast		2,600	2,680	2,760	4,160	5,350	5,350
Ballast Ratio		32.5%	40%	40%	40%	40%	40%
Sail Area, Square Feet		419	500	500	600	700	700/725
Sail Area-Displacement Ratio		16.76	22.5	22.1	20.15	19.83	19.83/20.54
Prismatic Coefficient		.614	.58	.60	.56	.63	.63
Pounds Per Inch Immersion		659			906	983	983
Auxiliary, Horsepower		9	9	9	18	27	27
Water, Gallons		40	25	25	100	110	110
Fuel, Gallons		25	25	25	40	55	55
Headroom		5'3"/6'1"	6'-1"	6'-1"	6'-3½"	6'-4"	6'-4"

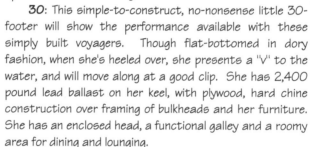

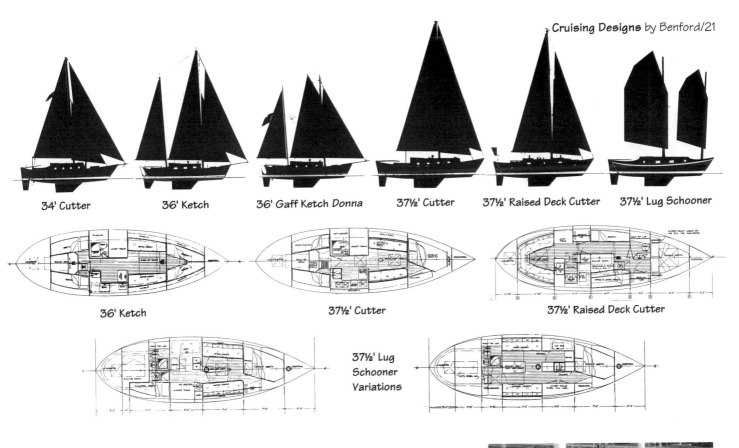

34' Cutter   36' Ketch   36' Gaff Ketch Donna   37½' Cutter   37½' Raised Deck Cutter   37½' Lug Schooner

36' Ketch   37½' Cutter   37½' Raised Deck Cutter

37½' Lug Schooner Variations

professional shop who'd like to set up for plywood production on a practical basis. She's slightly longer and narrower on deck than the 30' Sailing Dory, with which she shares her ketch rig, keel and construction details.

34: **Badger** is the best known of this design. Pete and Annie Hill built her on the proverbial shoestring, producing a very nice and creditable voyager. Annie has written a delightful and informative book about this, **Voyaging On A Small Income**, in which she details how they are able to keep on voyaging on a **very** small income. This is must reading for anyone who wants to spend their life cruising.

36: This relatively light displacement sailing dory with her 5,000 pounds of ballasted keel will move along at a most respectable pace, and still maintain a good deal of stability and solid comfort for her crew. Designed for offshore cruising and simplicity of construction, this practical vessel has very livable accommodations. Quarter berths aft will be most comfortable in a seaway. The head with shower and oilskin locker is conveniently close to the cockpit, and U-shaped galley to starboard. A full-size chart table is next to the enclosed head, with settee-berths midships around drop leaf table. The foc'sle is home to V-berths, or an optional double berth, and the chain locker in the forepeak. There's good amount of stowage space throughout the vessel, especially in the large lazarette.

37½: This is a variation of the 36-footer, with a little more length on deck. They share keels, structural drawings and many of the accommodation variation ideas are interchangeable. It has lug schooner and cutter rigs available.

34' Badger

36' Gaff Ketch Donna

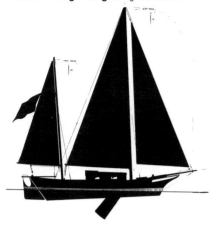

Shoal Draft Cruisers
27' Flattie & 40' Skipjack
Designs Number 82 & 43
1972 & 1967

These two traditional Chesapeake Bay type sail boats offer a combination of classic styling and good cruising accommodations. If you cruise in shallow waters, these boats have a lot to offer.

As her name implies, this 27' Flattie has a flat bottom extending aft from the bow, which Vee's from amidships to the stern. The rakish low freeboard emphasizes the graceful sheer. A simply constructed plywood vessel, she will prove a handsome addition to the fleet in any shallow water cruising grounds. Her sitting headroom cabin has a double berth in the bow, settee/berth and quarter berth to starboard, lounging seat over bucket amidships to port and stove/counter to port just forward of the long cockpit. She'll be a fast little sailer and a fine week-ender. For very light airs, she even has an optional spinnaker.

The 40' Skipjack offers good performance in light airs and under power with a small inboard. She sleeps six in three cabins. There's a raised convertible dinette and galley in the deckhouse.

A second version has a fixed, shallow draft keel instead of the centerboard and a bit more depth in the hull for more room in the cabins. With this version, the pilothouse is high enough to give visibility over the bow, thus giving the option of having inside an steering station. Plans are available for building either the plywood or steel versions with the keel or centerboard. Either way, she's a very comfortable cruiser!

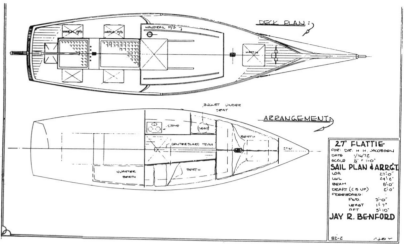

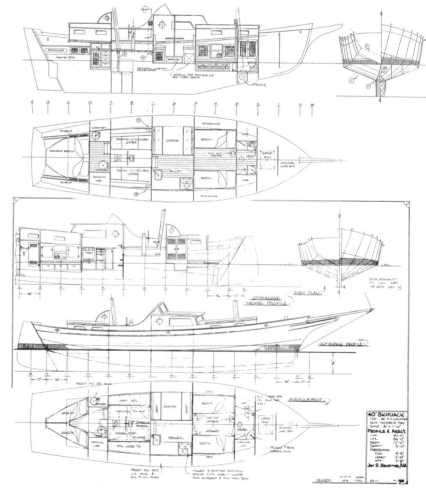

Particulars:	27	40 (CB)	40 (Keel)
Length overall	27'-0"	40'-0"	40'-0"
Length designed waterline	24'-2"	36'-0"	36'-0"
Beam	8'-0"	12'-0"	12'-0"
Draft, (C.B. Up/Down)	2'-0"/5'-6"	3'-0"/7'1"	4'-6"
Freeboard:			
Forward	3'-0"	4'-3"	4'-9"
Least	1'-7"	2'-0"	2'-6"
Aft	3'-10"	2'-9"	3'-3"
Displacement, cruising trim	4,750	18,400	26,000
Displacement-length ratio	150	176	249
Ballast	1200	5,500	6,500
Ballast ratio	25%	30%	30%
Sail area, sq. ft.	400	1,090	1,090
Sail area-displacement ratio	22.65	25.02	19.87
Prismatic coefficient		.62	.59
Tankage, water/fuel, gals.	Portable	100/100	100/100
Headroom	4'-10"	6'-5"	6'-5"

35' C. B. Ketch

36' C. B. Ketch

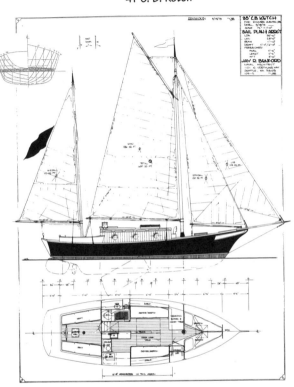

41' C. B. Ketch

Presto-type Ketches

Designs Number 105, 188 & 89
1973, 1977 & 1972

Many years ago Vincent Gilpin wrote a delightful book called **The Good Little Ship**. It extolled the virtues of the **Presto**-type centerboarders which have proven able and seaworthy boats in all conditions.

These attractive gaff ketches started out with the **Presto**-type in mind, and evolved to meet our clients' varying needs. The 35 and 36 have V-berths in the bow; a drawing board and/or chart table opposite the hanging locker slightly aft; settee/berths amidships around the drop-leaf table which is over the C.B. trunk; U-shaped galley to starboard and head with shower to port. There's good headroom in main cabin area. There is also a comfortable long cockpit aft.

The 41 has an aft cabin for separation of the crew into fore and aft quarters. It also has larger storage in the ends, or the bow can have a couple pipe berths. She also has a gaff mizzen and single headsail rig.

Particulars:		35'	36'	41'
Length overall		35'-0"	36'-0"	41'-0"
Length designed waterline		28'-0"	28'-0"	35'-0"
Beam		11'-0"	11'-0"	12'-0"
Draft	(C.B. Up/Down)	2'-6"/6'-0"	2'-6"/6'-0"	2'-6"/6'-3"
Freeboard:	Forward	4'-6"	4'-9"	5'-0"
	Least	2'-6"	2'-9"	2'-6"
	Aft	3'-0"	3'-9"	3'-3"
Displacement, cruising trim, lbs.		15,750	13,800	20,670
Displacement-length ratio		320	281	215
Ballast			4,400 lbs.	
Sail area, sq. ft.		600	600	894
Sail area-displacement ratio		15.3	16.7	19.0
Prismatic coefficient		.51	.55	.56
Tankage, fuel/water, gals.			30/100	
Headroom		6'-5"	6'-2"	6'-3"

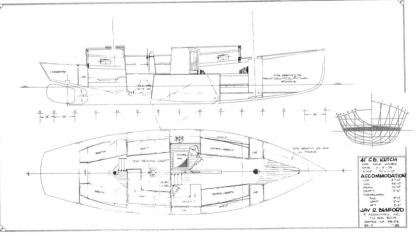

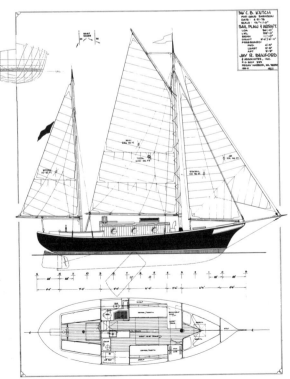

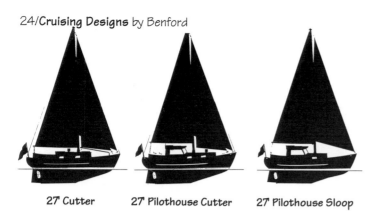

27 Cutter 27 Pilothouse Cutter 27 Pilothouse Sloop

Offshore Double-Enders
27' Cutter & Pilothouse Cutter/Sloop
Design number 124
1975

This handsome cutter can be thought of as a bigger version of the Benford 22 Knockabout. She's a fast and responsive sailer with good ability to carry sail in a blow.

The Cutter has a big double berth forward, open main saloon, with settees port and starboard, the port one making into another berth. There is a good sized chart table, galley, and enclosed head with room for shower. She has 6'-2" headroom in her cabin.

The Pilothouse Cutter has two raised seats in the pilothouse, one of which is at the inside helm. The settees extend back under the raised sole, at the seats in the pilothouse, to make them usable as berths. They also have extension pieces to make them wider. The head is in the bow, forward of the galley.

The Pilothouse Sloop has a different cabin layout, with the Cutter's double berth forward and settee to port that makes into upper and lower berths. Her enclosed head and galley are along the starboard side of the saloon. She also has raised seats in the pilothouse, so that there is room for two to sit inside and operate the boat, out of the weather.

These three variations have but scratched the surface of the possibilities for interior arrangement plans. Let us know how you'd like your version laid out.

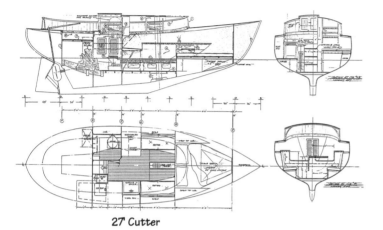

27' Cutter

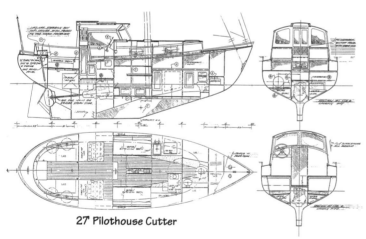

27' Pilothouse Cutter

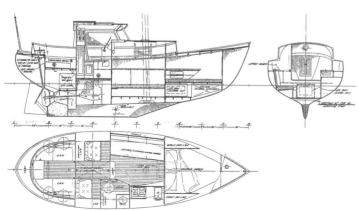

27' Pilothouse Sloop

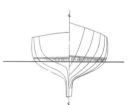

Particulars:

Length overall		27'-0"
Length designed waterline		22'-6"
Beam		8'-9½"
Draft		4'-0"
Freeboard:	Forward	4'-4½"
	Least	2'-8"
	Aft	3'-9½"
Displacement, cruising trim		9,235 lbs.
Displacement-length ratio		362
Ballast		3080 lbs.
Ballast ratio		33%
Sail area		450 sq. ft.
Sail area-displacement ratio		16.4
Prismatic coefficient		.544
Pounds per inch immersion		638
Entrance half-angle		23°
Water tankage		45 Gals.
Fuel tankage		30-40 Gals.
Headroom		6'-2"

Offshore Double-Enders
30' D. E. Cutter & 32' D. E. Auxiliary Ketch/Cutter
Designs Number 74 & 56
1971 & 1969

These two double-enders offer a study in contrasts in how to achieve a good seagoing vessel. The 30-footer gets her stability from having a lot of ballast and locating it very low. Her heavy displacement will make for dampened motion on long passages. The 32-footer uses her hull form to get more stability with less ballast and less draft. She will be a bit stiffer. Both will have similar load-carrying ability

Capable of extended offshore cruising and passage making, the handsome 30' Double-Ended Cutter sleeps five and could be a suitable home afloat for a couple. Her forward stateroom could have a double berth. Her shape makes her a relatively easy boat to build. This plan is available with metric dimensioning in addition to our standard of feet-and-inches.

A high performance, light displacement boat with midship cockpit, the 32' Auxiliary Ketch offers private accommodations for two couples for coastwise cruising. A comfortable dinette converts to a double berth, with functional galley and head all in forward cabin. Large double berth & lockers are in aft private cabin. She's built strip planked on bulkheads, and her round bilge hull has 3,000 pounds of lead ballast on the keel.

The 32' Auxiliary Cutter version has an aft cockpit and a large, roomy main cabin. There is a U-shaped galley out of the traffic, a chart table handy to the cockpit, and settee-berths either side of a large drop-leaf table. The enclosed head has room for a shower and the forward cabin has a good sized double berth. Her handy, all inboard cutter rig has a variety of sail combinations available for driving her in all conditions.

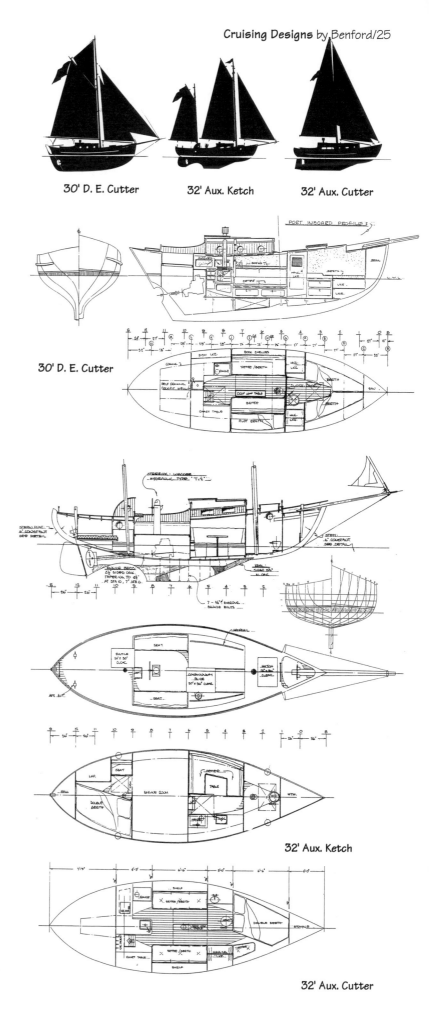

30' D. E. Cutter • 32' Aux. Ketch • 32' Aux. Cutter

30' D. E. Cutter

32' Aux. Ketch

32' Aux. Cutter

Particulars:		74	56 (Ketch/Cutter)
Length Overall		30'-0"	32'-0"
Length Designed Waterline		27'-0"	26'-0"
Beam		9'-6"	10'-7"
Draft		5'-0"	4'-0"
Freeboard:	Forward	4'-6"	5'-3½"
	Least	2'-3"	2'-10½"
	Aft	3'-3"	3'-9"
Displacement, Cruising Trim		19,000 lbs.	10,700 lbs.
Displacement-Length Ratio		431	272
Ballast		9,000 lbs.	3,000 lbs.
Ballast Ratio		47%	28%
Sail Area, Square Feet		608	525/560
Sail Area-Displacement Ratio		13.66	17.30/18.45
Prismatic Coefficient		.5	.54
Pounds Per Inch Immersion		865	880
Entrance Half-Angle		26°	25°
Water/Fuel Tankage, Gals.		70/50	30-100/30-100
Headroom		5'-9" to 6'-7"	6'-1½"/6'-5"

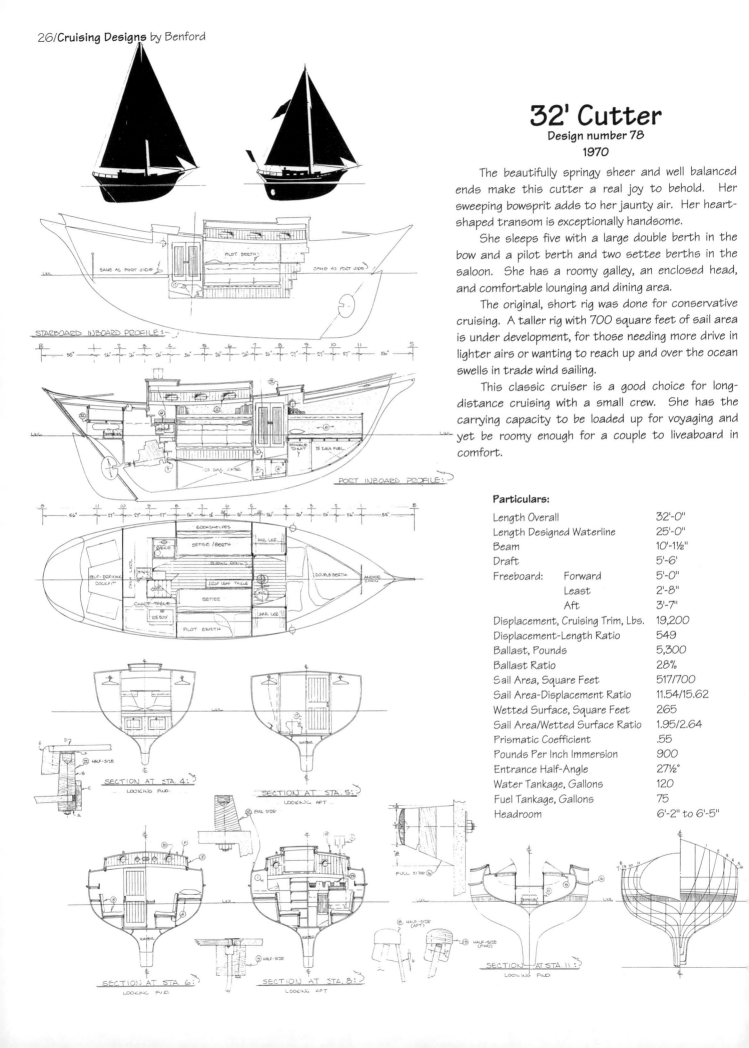

32' Cutter
Design number 78
1970

The beautifully springy sheer and well balanced ends make this cutter a real joy to behold. Her sweeping bowsprit adds to her jaunty air. Her heart-shaped transom is exceptionally handsome.

She sleeps five with a large double berth in the bow and a pilot berth and two settee berths in the saloon. She has a roomy galley, an enclosed head, and comfortable lounging and dining area.

The original, short rig was done for conservative cruising. A taller rig with 700 square feet of sail area is under development, for those needing more drive in lighter airs or wanting to reach up and over the ocean swells in trade wind sailing.

This classic cruiser is a good choice for long-distance cruising with a small crew. She has the carrying capacity to be loaded up for voyaging and yet be roomy enough for a couple to liveaboard in comfort.

Particulars:

Length Overall		32'-0"
Length Designed Waterline		25'-0"
Beam		10'-1½"
Draft		5'-6'
Freeboard:	Forward	5'-0"
	Least	2'-8"
	Aft	3'-7"
Displacement, Cruising Trim, Lbs.		19,200
Displacement-Length Ratio		549
Ballast, Pounds		5,300
Ballast Ratio		28%
Sail Area, Square Feet		517/700
Sail Area-Displacement Ratio		11.54/15.62
Wetted Surface, Square Feet		265
Sail Area/Wetted Surface Ratio		1.95/2.64
Prismatic Coefficient		.55
Pounds Per Inch Immersion		900
Entrance Half-Angle		27½°
Water Tankage, Gallons		120
Fuel Tankage, Gallons		75
Headroom		6'-2" to 6'-5"

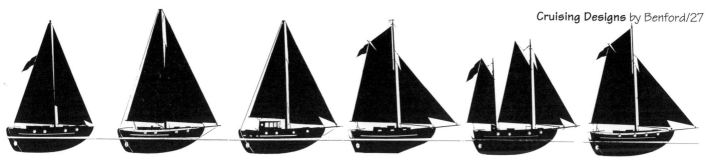

Mercedes
35' Colin Archer Type Cutter or Ketch
Design number 77
1971

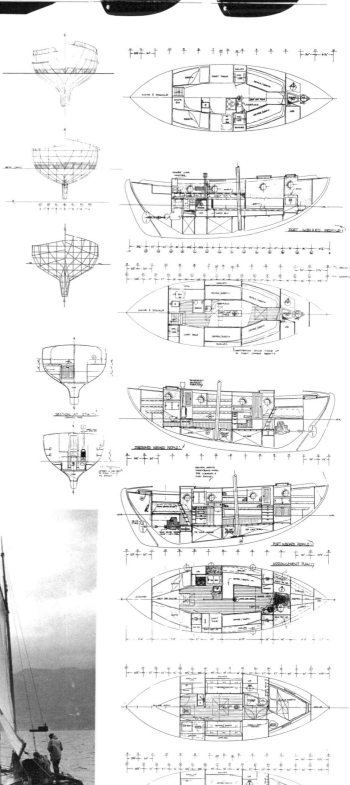

This flush-decked, double-ender is among the easier round-bilged shapes to build and outfit. A good liveaboard for two, there is a choice of several interior arrangements, and either gaff cutter, Marconi cutter, or gaff ketch rigs. Refined from a rugged, highly seaworthy shape, she is among our most popular designs.

The original wineglass shape has been modified for one of the cold-molded versions into a 6" shallower draft hull with a solid timber and ballast keel. This form could also be used with the 'glass versions. A multi-chine version has also been done as an alternative for building the boat in steel in either round or chine form. The wineglass shape has the most room for tankage and storage with the extra volume in the bilge area.

In 1982 one of these 35-footers made a record-setting 286-day non-stop singlehanded circumnavigation. Our client wrote us, "Your 'Benford 35' (ketch rigged) design, built....in Holland, proved to be very much the boat I needed for this (sometimes) spartanic trip. Both ship and rigging stood up to my high expectations and in this case one could say: 'You can't argue with success'....I CAN'T AGREE MORE."

One of our most popular designs, the multitude of layouts and rigs makes for a great variety of possible versions. Which one would be best for you?

Particulars:

Length overall		35'-0"
Length designed waterline		30'-0"
Beam		11'-6"
Draft		5'-6"
Freeboard:	Forward	5'-0"
	Least	3'-9"
	Aft	3'-11"
Displacement, Cruising Trim		23,240 lbs.
Displacement-Length Ratio		383
Ballast		10,000 lbs.
Ballast Ratio		43%
Sail Area, Sq. Ft./Sail Area-Displ. Ratio:		
Cutter		700/13.75
Gaff cutter		740/14.54
Ketch		753/14.79
Prismatic Coefficient		.538
Pounds Per Inch Immersion		1,035
Entrance Half-Angle		23¾°
Water Tankage		160 Gals.
Fuel Tankage		65 Gals.
Headroom		6'-2½"

Dawn

Dawn

Sunrise

Sunrise with Great Pyramid Rig

Sunrise

Sunrise & Dawn
34' & 32' Pinky Ketches
Design Number 92 & 202
1972 & 1981

Sunrise was my home for a decade and proved to be a very comfortable and capable cruiser, plus a splendid liveaboard. Her traditional New England Pinky type hull is carries a square topsail ketch rig to make her a lovely — and lively — sight under sail. A comfortable offshore cruiser for two (or a couple with one or two children) she is laid out with double berth forward, settee-berths and drop-leaf table amidships, galley at the aft end of the saloon, large chart table and head with shower. The aft end of the vessel devoted to engine room and cockpit space. The Great Pyramid (square) Rig is ideal for setting many different combinations of sails with minimal effort to keep her going well in a large variety of wind conditions. All sails can be handled from on deck.

Dawn is a smaller version, designed about a decade later with many of the ideas of how to do this refined over thousands of miles and hours of cruising on **Sunrise**. **Dawn**'s accommodations has the double/master stateroom aft, with a nice skylight on the large bridgedeck for light and ventilation. The galley, head, chart table, and settee-berths are laid out in the manner that worked so well on **Sunrise**, except that the settees form a dead-end social area that permits leaving the table up all the time, if wanted. **Dawn**'s hull has a foot less draft, without the wineglass shaped sections of **Sunrise**. This helps give her good stability too, with good sail carrying power.

Particulars:	202	92
Length overall	35'-0"	38'-0"
Length on deck	32'-0"	34'-6"
Length designed waterline	29'-0"	30'-8"
Beam	11'-0"	11'-3"
Draft	5'-0"	6'-3"
Freeboard: Forward	4'-6"	4'-2½"
Least	2'-6"	2'-3½"
Aft	3'-6"	3'-4½"
Displacement, cruising trim, lbs.	18,900	31,240
Displacement-length ratio	342	479
Ballast, pounds	6,750	10,300
Ballast ratio	36%	33%
Sail area, square feet	800	1238
Sail area-displacement ratio	18.04	19.97
Prismatic coefficient	.55	.577
Pounds per inch immersion	982	1,200
Entrance half-angle	22½°	25°
Water tankage, gallons	120	125
Fuel tankage, gallons	60	108
Headroom	6'-5"	6'-2"

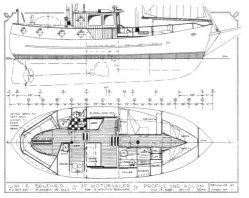

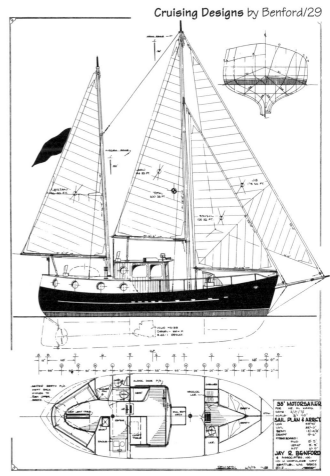

35' Motorsailer
Design number 87
1971

The motorsailer version of **Strumpet** was created for a client that wanted the character and charm of **Strumpet**, with the addition of considerably increased accommodations aft and an auxiliary sailing rig. She has also been built without the rig as a great cabin motoryacht. Deep bulwarks like **Strumpet** make her a secure working platform.

A head tucks under a seat in the forward cabin. There's a larger chart table in the pilothouse, and the aft cabin is the social area. The settees in the stern convert to uppers and lowers and surround a large drop-leaf table in the great cabin. Part of the generous galley is tucked under the chart table in the pilothouse, increasing the counter space available. The head is quite roomy, and has a separate shower stall.

An alternative version is available with additional cabin accommodations in the cargo hold area. For those desiring more emphasis on her sailing performance, we could adapt one of our larger sail plans from another design (like **Corcovado**) to give a full size sailing rig. Call us to discuss this idea.

Tankage provides for 600 gallons of fuel oil and 200 of water. With a variable pitch prop hooked to a small diesel, she can have a cruising range of about 4,000 miles at 6 knots. This can make her a real passagemaker, and for more information about this type of boat, Robert P. Beebe's book, **Voyaging Under Power**, is the best source of information.

Sukekazu Nagata's 35' Motorsailer, **Dai San Kuroshio Maru** (which means **Black Current Circle III**), gliding gracefully along. She was built in Himeji City, Japan, and with the exception of the stern pulpit, her exterior appears to be built faithfully to the original design.

Particulars of 35' Motorsailer:

Length overall		35'-0"
Length designed waterline		32'-0"
Beam		12'-4½"
Draft		4'-6"
Freeboard:	Forward	5'-9"
	Least	3'-3"
	Aft	6'-0"
Displacement, cruising trim*		27,900 lbs.
Displacement-length ratio		380
Sail area		600 sq. ft.
Sail area-displacement ratio		10.44
Prismatic coefficient		0.634
Pounds per inch immersion		1,420
Water		200 gals.
Fuel		600 gals.
Headroom		6'-6"

***CAUTION:** The figure for displacement quoted here is for the boat in cruising trim. That is, with the fuel and water tanks filled, the crew on board, as well as the crews' gear and stores in the lockers. This should not be confused with the "shipping weight" often quoted as "displacement" by some manufacturers. This should be taken into account when comparing figure and ratios between this and other designs.

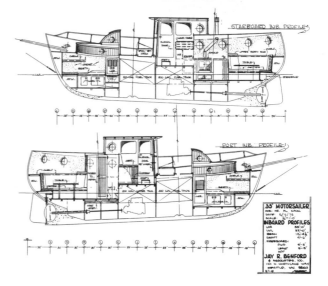

Corcovado
37' Pilothouse Cutter or Ketch
Design Number 125 & 209
1975 & 1983

Corcovado is a very successful marriage of an efficient cruising cutter and the traditional motorsailer. She sails like a thoroughbred cruiser yet provides the comforts and amenities of a traditional motorsailer. These include private staterooms fore and aft, roomy social area, galley and head, all amidships, and an extremely well lit pilothouse with settees both sides of the steering station. All of this combined into a handsome and salty package.

A larger sister (in hull form) to our 35' trawler **Strumpet**, with lead ballasted keel, she has extensive interior accommodations for a vessel her size. This is enhanced by the extended trunk cabin, yet does not detract from the spacious self-draining cockpit aft from

where fishing and working the ship in more pleasant weather will be most enjoyable, in this alternate version.

The second version of this hull design is a double chine hull form designed for building in steel. It could also be used for aluminum with the construction plans modified.

After a trip to Alaska and back in the summer of 1980, *Corcovado*'s owner said, "The design you did on *Corcovado* pleases us very much....We have sailed with jib, staysail and main and have hit as high as 8½ knots. I feather the prop and can pick up another knot or two if we are moving in a 20 to 25 mph wind....With all gear and supplies on board our waterline is right on as computed by you."

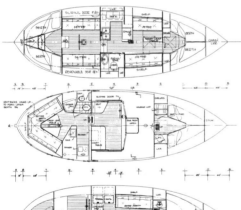

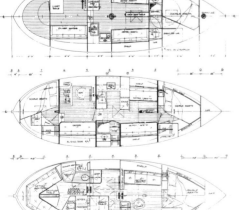

Particulars:

Length overall	37'-0"
Length designed waterline	33'-0"
Beam	12'-4"
Draft	5'-0"
Freeboard:	
Forward	5'-9"
Least	3'-3"
Aft	4'-3"
Displacement, cruising trim	28,450 lbs.
Displacement-length ratio	353
Ballast	7,100 lbs.
Ballast ratio	25%
Sail area	800/900 ft.²
Sail area-displacement ratio	13.73/15.45
Prismatic coefficient	.619
Pounds per inch immersion	1,468
Entrance half-angle	29°
Water tankage	180 Gals.
Fuel tankage	200 Gals.
Headroom	6'-3"
GM	4.3'

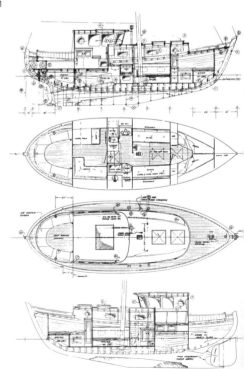

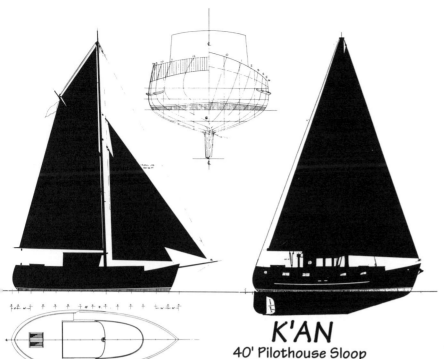

K'AN
40' Pilothouse Sloop
Design Number 147
1977

Conceived as an expanded and improved version of our 37' *Corcovado*, this 40-footer has proved to be an excellent all weather cruiser. Like the 37, she has a long keel that is a distinct appendage, shaped like a full length NACA-sectioned fin. This has proved to be very effective in providing good lateral resistance with moderate draft.

The are two rig choices for her — the efficient masthead Marconi cutter rig and the romantic gaff cutter with a topsail. The gaff rig is a more low-tech solution and can be done with a grown stick and simply fabricated hardware and fittings.

The powering is done with an efficient Hundested variable pitch propeller for making the most effective use of the combined powerplant and sailing rig to drive her easily.

K'AN is the Haida Indian word for dolphin. After watching her underway, it seems like she is well named. She has a clean wake and uses very low power to get her to cruising speed. Combined with her spacious accommodations, this makes for a great cruiser.

K'AN running cleanly at launching-day trials.

Particulars:

Length overall		40'-0"
Length designed waterline		36'-0"
Beam		14'-0"
Draft		5'-6"
Freeboard:	Forward	6'-6"
	Least	3'-3¼"
	Aft	6'-0"
Displacement, cruising trim		30,795 lbs.
Displacement-length ratio		295
Ballast		7,700 lbs.
Ballast ratio		25%
Sail area Marconi/Gaff, Sq. Ft.		921/1,000
Sail area-displacement ratio		15.0/16.3
Wetted surface		482 sq. ft.
Sail area-wetted surface ratio		1.91/2.07
Prismatic coefficient		.56
Pounds per inch immersion		1,658
Entrance half-angle		25°
Water tankage		205 Gals.
Fuel tankage		120 Gals.
Headroom		6'-2½"-6'-6"
GM		4.14'

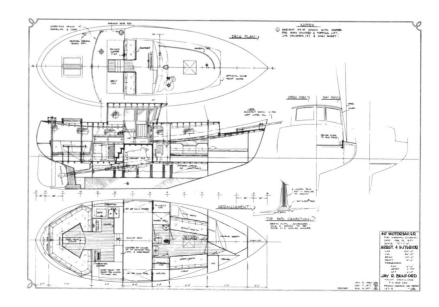

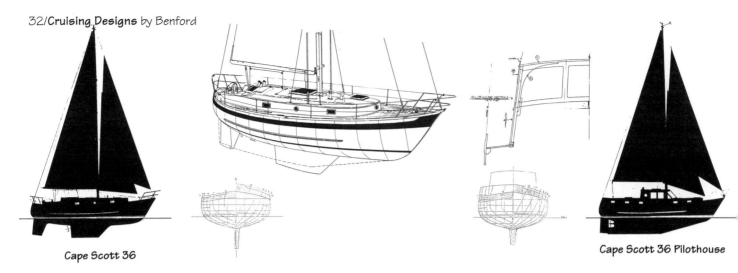

Cape Scott 36

Cape Scott 36 Pilothouse

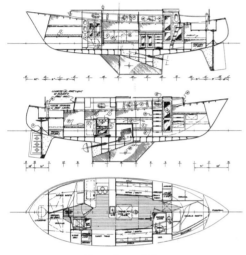

Cape Scott 36

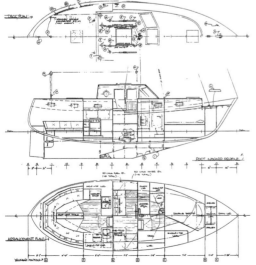

Cape Scott 36 Pilothouse

Offshore Double Enders
Cape Scott 36, Cascade Classic 39 & 40' Cutter & Pilothouse Cutter
Designs Number 162, 222, 159, & 166
1977, 1984, 1977 & 1977

These are well proven seaboats, with many voyages behind them. They are modern, medium-displacement cruisers. They're fast, stiff, weatherly and easily driven, yet their long, shallow keels make for simple solutions to maintenance in far-off ports. Their accommodations combine the best of the most popular and practical cruising boats. The roomy layouts include double staterooms fore and aft (a convertible settee in the pilothouse version), large storage in the ends, a good working chart table, large galley, head with shower, and a large saloon amidships.

The 39 is available as a molded 'glass hull and deck (or finished boat) and the 36 and 40 are done as one-offs with choices of either an aft cockpit or pilothouse version. The pilothouse has been adapted onto the 39 for those wanting a 'glass kit.

The 36 has an alternative fin keel, with a bit deeper draft, for those in pursuit of the last bit of light air performance. The pilothouse 36 has a roomy great cabin which makes a comfortable saloon. This 36 has made several single-handed trips from Puget Sound to Alaska.

These offshore double enders are a good size for a couple or a family to live and cruise aboard. They are of a size that is roomy enough to carry long term stores and not be crowded for daily living.

Particulars:		36	36PH	39	40	40PH
Length overall		36'-0"	36'-0"	39'-0"	40'-0"	40'-0"
Length designed waterline		31'-0"	31'-0'	34'-0"	35'-0"	35'-0"
Beam		12'-0"	12'-0'	12'-4"	12'-4"	12'-4"
Draft		5'-4"	4'-6"	5'-0"	5'-0"	5'-0"
Freeboard:	Forward	5'-6"	5'-6"	5'-6"	5'-6"	5'-6"
	Least	3'-6"	3'-6"	3'-3"	3'-6"	3'-6"
	Aft	4'-3"	5'-6"	4'-3"	4'-3"	4'-3"
Displacement, cruising trim, lbs.		17,000	18,180	23,275	23,900	23,900
Displacement-length ratio		255	272	264	249	249
Ballast, lbs.		6,000	6,000	8,000	8,500	8,500
Ballast ratio		35%	33%	34%	36%	36%
Sail area, square feet		725	725	848	871	849
Sail area-displacement ratio		17.55	16.78	16.64	16.80	16.38
Prismatic coefficient		.556	.542	.557	.557	.557
Pounds per inch immersion		1,185	1,185	1,367	1,380	1,380
Entrance half-angle		25°	25°	24¼°	22°	22°
Tankage, water/fuel, gals.		84/60	100/100	200/100	100/100	119/300
Headroom		6'-8"	6'-5"	6'-8"	6'-8"	6'-5"

Cascade Classic 39

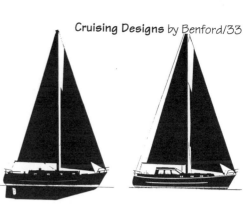

40' D. E. Cutter   40' Pilothouse Cutter

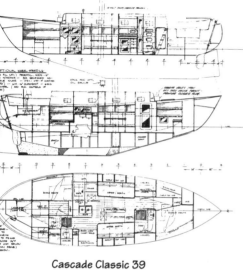

Cascade Classic 39

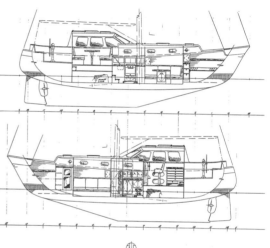

The cockpit of the Cascade
Classic 39 (above) shows how
her seatbacks are tall and well
shaped and sloped for the
comfort and safety of the crew.
Her galley and saloon
(below) show the spacious and
comfortable spaces found inside
to make life pleasant for her crew.

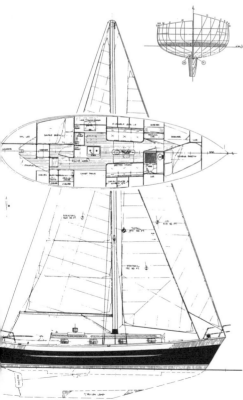

40' D. E. Cutter

40' Pilothouse Cutter

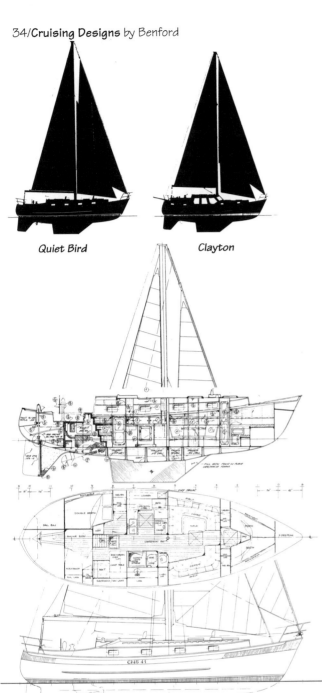

Quiet Bird   Clayton

Quiet Bird

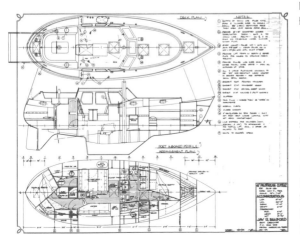

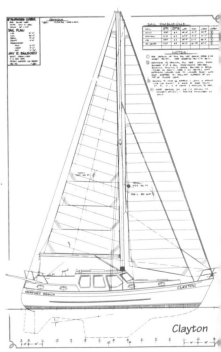

Quiet Bird
41' Double Ended Cutter & Pilothouse Cutter
Design Number 156
1977

Quiet Bird is a very successful offshore double ender. She's made fast passage-making a fine art. She is one of the many boats built to this design. They've proven to be fast, stiff and weatherly. What more can one ask of a good offshore cruiser?...

Her design is the result of our being commissioned to produce a production design based on the combination of our experience in living aboard and our work in producing fast cruisers. The result has been a pleasure to all and a comfort to those living aboard.

Since the fiberglass ones went out of production, we've created alternate cold-molded versions of both the fin keel version and a 5' draft, long keel, great cabin version, for voyaging in waters a bit shallower.

Clayton is the pilothouse version. It offers the option of inside steering with shelter from the sun and rain. The raised saloon provides a good view of the world around you while still seated inside. Being able to watch the horizon like this is a great help to those bothered by motion sickness. Clayton also offers private double berth staterooms with their own heads with shower stalls at either end of the boat. The generously sized galley is a couple steps down and forward of the raised saloon. The storage that is usually in the lazarette is now in a large bow locker, featuring many built-in shelves.

Particulars:

Length overall		41'-0"
Length designed waterline		36'-0"
Beam		14'-0"
Draft		6'-0"
Freeboard:	Forward	6'-0"
	Least	3'-6"
	Aft	4'-6"
Displacement, cruising trim		26,000 lbs.
Displacement-length ratio		249
Ballast		8,300 lbs.
Ballast ratio		32%
Sail area		949 sq. ft.
Sail area-displacement ratio		17.30
Prismatic coefficient		.547
Pounds per inch immersion		1,552
Entrance half-angle		22¼°
Water tankage		300 Gals.
Fuel tankage		100 Gals.
Headroom		6'-10"

Clayton

40' Steel Brigantine

Design Number 129
1975

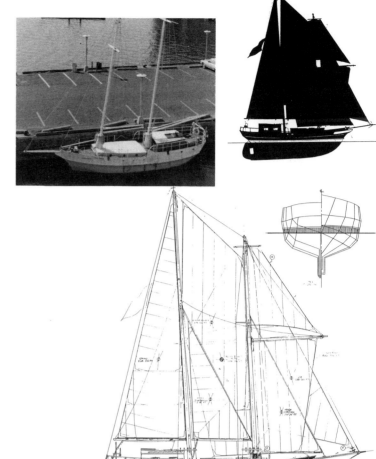

How do those long-distance cruisers keep their finances in order? Are they independently wealthy? Or do they work as they go to keep up some cash flow? Many keep cruising by doing the latter — they work during breaks in their cruising. One way to do this is to carry the tools of their trade aboard.

This 40' Brigantine was designed for a cruising couple where the husband was a machinist and wanted a small machine shop on board. The equipment weight, the parts and tools associated with it and the steel structure of the boat necessitated a heavy displacement design. The benefits are a wonderfully easy motion and steady feeling which those used to lightweight coastal cruisers will find amazing.

The aft deckhouse has the owners' double berth, a lounging seat and an inside steering station with chart table. Down a few steps and walking through the engine room/machine shop takes one to the forward cabin. There, amidships, is the head next to the companionway ladder, making access for the on deck watch easy. The galley and dinette are good sized with plenty of storage spaces.

The forward cabin has v-berths, which could be converted to a double berth with locker opposite. In the bow is another locker and chain locker.

Her rig is staysail schooner, with a square yard on the foremast, making her a brigantine. She could be sailed without the square rig as a schooner, or the rig could be slightly modified like The Great Pyramid Rig on **Sunrise**, which has proven very effective and easily handled with a small crew.

Her hull form takes the knuckle from the fantail stern forward as a topside chine and the widest part of the boat amidships. This can be built with a section of pipe built in here to make a sturdy guard rail. A handsome ship which will make life aboard pleasant for her crew, she will make for an interesting lifestyle for years to come.

Particulars:

Length overall		40'-0"
Length designed waterline		32'-0"
Beam		11'-0"
Draft		6'-0"
Freeboard:	Forward	5'-1"
	Least	3'-4"
	Aft	4'-0½"
Displacement, cruising trim		37,120 lbs.
Displacement-length ratio		498
Ballast		12,000 lbs.
Ballast ratio		32%
Sail area		1,100 sq. ft.
Sail area-displacement ratio		15.86
Prismatic coefficient		.635
Pounds per inch immersion		1,366
Entrance half-angle		26°
Water tankage		250 Gals.
Fuel tankage		150 Gals.
Headroom		6'-3"

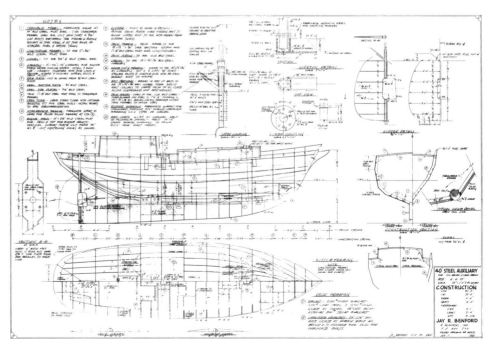

42' Coasting Schooner

42' La Flaneuse

42' Sq. Tops'l Schooner

42' South Seas Trader

42' Alaskan Trader

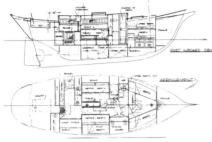

42' Coasting Schooner

42' Square Topsail Schooner

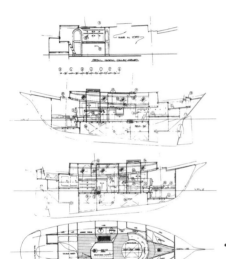

42' Topsail Schooner — La Flaneuse

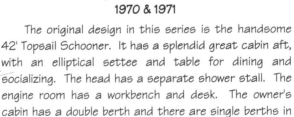

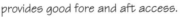

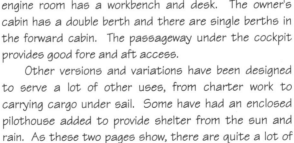

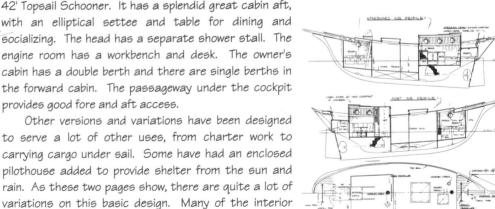

The Benford 42/43 Series

Designs Number 57 & 75
1970 & 1971

The original design in this series is the handsome 42' Topsail Schooner. It has a splendid great cabin aft, with an elliptical settee and table for dining and socializing. The head has a separate shower stall. The engine room has a workbench and desk. The owner's cabin has a double berth and there are single berths in the forward cabin. The passageway under the cockpit provides good fore and aft access.

Other versions and variations have been designed to serve a lot of other uses, from charter work to carrying cargo under sail. Some have had an enclosed pilothouse added to provide shelter from the sun and rain. As these two pages show, there are quite a lot of variations on this basic design. Many of the interior and rigs can be interchanged in whole or in part to create even more versions.

Many of the schooner rigs are variations on the topsail schooner, with or without the topmasts and squaresail yards. Similarly, the 42/43 ketches are available with and without the topmasts and yards.

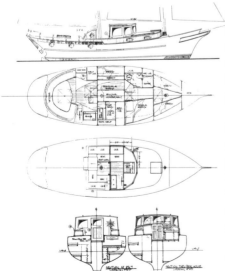

42' Schooner — Pilothouse Version

42' Trading Schooner — South Seas Trader

42' Trading Schooner — Alaskan Trader

42' Marconi Ketch

42' Square Topsail Ketch

43' Gaff Ketch

43' Motorsailer #1

43' Motorsailer #2

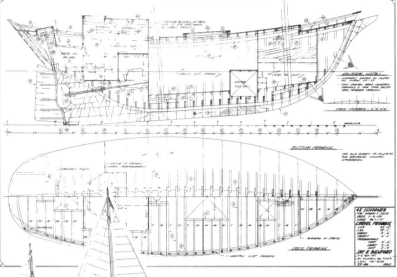

⇦ *The wood construction plan at left is one of the many detail sheets for this design.*

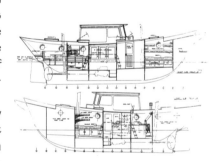

43' Gaff Ketch

The 43-footer is a variation on the original 42' hull with the break in the sheer line eliminated and this higher sheer carried out to the new bow length with the resulting gain of 6" of length. The 43 is also available with the keel shortened to give a draft of 5' instead of 6'. In addition to the round bilge hull there is a multi-chine version for building in steel.

Many boats have been built from these plans. They have proven to be very good seaboats, fast passagemakers and as comfortable for long ocean passages as for living aboard in port. From her heart-shaped transom to her clipper bow she's a classic and has proven to be the heart's desire of many delighted cruising families.

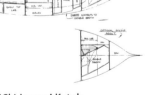

43' Motorsailer #1

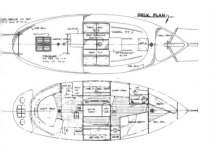

42' Marconi Ketch

42' Sq. Tops'l Ketch

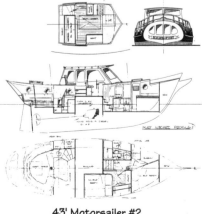

43' Motorsailer #2

Particulars:		#57	Steel	#75
Length overall		42'-6"	42'-6"	43'-0"
Length designed waterline		32'-0"	32'-0"	32'-8"
Beam		13'-6"	13'-5½"	13'-6"
Draft		6'-0"	6'-0"	5'-0"
Freeboard:	Forward	6'-6"	6'-6"	7'-1"
	Least	3'-4"	3'-4"	3'-9½"
	Aft	5'-4"	5'-4"	5'-1"
Displacement, cruising trim, lbs.		36,000	33,000	39,000
Displacement-length ratio		490	450	499
Ballast, lbs.		10,800	9,000	10,800
Ballast ratio		30%	27%	28%
Sail area		Varies: 850 to 1,443 sq.ft.		
Sail area-displacement ratio		Varies: 12.05 to 22.44		
Prismatic coefficient		.56	.57	
Pounds per inch immersion		1,487 (Typical)		
Water tankage, Gals.		330	300	300
Fuel tankage, Gals.		160	165	250
Headroom		6'-6" to 6'-9" (Typical)		

44' & 45' Cat Ketches
Designs Number 184, 218, 219 & 192
1979, 1984 & 1980

The Boundary Bay 44 hull form has excellent form stability. Her firm bilges can be seen in the body plan, plus the long foil shape of the keel. We use this same foil shape for shorter fin keels, merely stretched out, and it gives good flow characteristics. I've used this shape with success on previous designs and found that it provides good windward performance on a boat with shallow draft. The modest draft will be well appreciated in gunkholing.

The forefoot is cut away to provide good response in maneuvering. Keel area is maintained aft to provide for good tracking and course keeping. The rudder area is ample and will provide for keeping her on course with small angles, thus minimizing the drag encountered by smaller rudders which have to be cranked over to much greater angles to steer the boats, with these large angles making the rudders act like brakes.

The stern is my favorite, giving a graceful and elegant appearance. It will also give a good account of itself in a seaway, lifting over the seas and parting them like a double ender. There is plenty of stern deck space and the deep bulwarks slope to make a nice backrest for lounging on deck.

The midships cockpit is also shaped for comfort. The backrests are all high enough to give good support, and are well sloped for comfort. The seats are fitted with drains that direct any accumulation of rain or spray down to the cockpit scuppers, instead of leaving puddles to be sat in.

Down below, the accommodation plan provides comfort and privacy for two couples, with space for more on the settees and quarter berth. With the staterooms at each end of the boat, there is good separation, and the head and galley are accessible without disturbing the occupants of the other stateroom.

The head and galley, as well as the navigation area, are directly off the companionway. This easy access from the cockpit will mean that the settees and salon won't get soaked with seawater every time someone comes off deck for something from the galley or the head.

Three variations on the 44 have been worked up. The first was the steel 45-footer, with some revisions to the interior as well. Next came the cold-molded, fin-keel version, using the original interior. Then, there is the double chine Airex® version, also using the original interior.

Another variation possible with these boats is the use of a cutter rig for those wanting a more conventional rig. Part of the fun of the design business for us is working on variations — doing a variety of boats and types keeps it interesting.

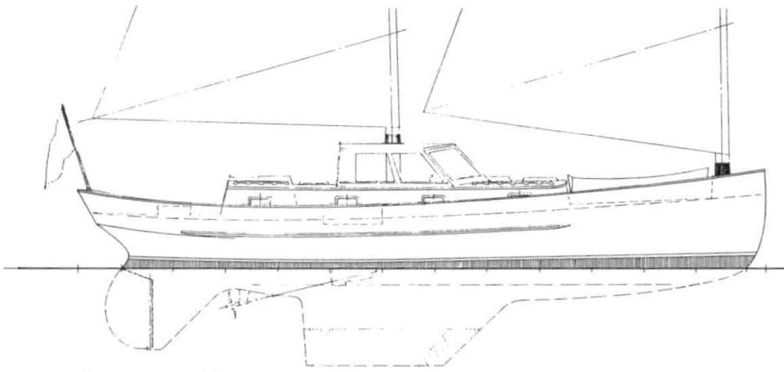

Fin Keel 44

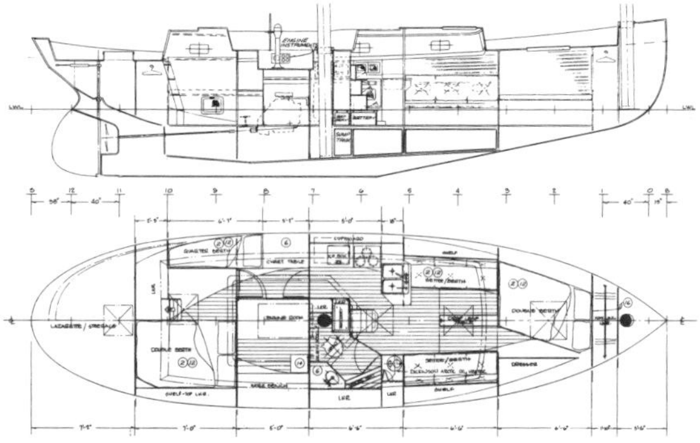

Boundary Bay 44

45' Cat Ketch

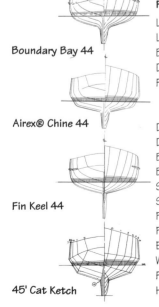

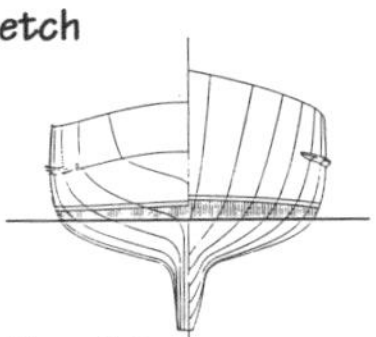

Boundary Bay 44

Airex® Chine 44

Fin Keel 44

45' Cat Ketch

Particulars :		BB44	Chine 44	Fin Keel 44	45' Cat K.	— Argonauta — Wood	Steel
Length overall		44'-0"	44'-0"	44'-0"	45'-0"	45'-0"	45'-0"
Length designed waterline		40'-0"	40'-0"	40'-0"	40'-0"	37'-6"	37'-6"
Beam		12'-0"	12'-0"	12'-0"	12'-0"	12'-3"	12'-6"
Draft		4'-6"	4'-6"	6'-0"	5'-0"	5'-0"	5'-0"
Freeboard:	Forward	6'-0¾"	6'-0¾"	6'-0¾"	6'-2½"	6'-6"	6'-6"
	Least	3'-9¾"	3'-9¾"	3'-9¾"	3'-9¾"	4'-6"	4'-6"
	Aft	4'-9¼"	4'-9¼"	4'-9¼"	4'-9¼"	5'-3"	5'-3"
Displacement, cruising trim, lbs.		22,850	25,100	19,800	30,420	24,475	29,400
Displacement-length ratio		159.5	175	138	212	207	249
Ballast, lbs.		8,000	8,000	6,500	7,600	8,000	8,000
Ballast ratio		35%	31%	33%	25%	33%	27%
Sail area, square feet		920	920	920	920	900	900
Sail area-displacement ratio		18.3	17.16	20.11	15.1	17.08	15.11
Prismatic coefficient		.526	.55	.544	.532	.536	.594
Pounds per inch immersion		1,450	1,450	1,450	1,540	1,352	1.514
Entrance half-angle		19°	20°	19°	20°	22½°	26°
Water tankage, gallons		160	160	160	160	90	150
Fuel tankage, gallons		75	75	75	75	100	150
Headroom		6'-4½"	6'-4½"	6'-4½"	6'-5"	6'-3"	6'-2" to 6'-8"

Argonauta
45' Fantail Cutter
Designs Number 195 & 215
1981 & 1984

Argonauta was designed for the well known marine artist and illustrator, Stephen L. Davis. The hull form is an evolutionary development of a series we've been working on for a while, some of which are shown on the preceeding page. (Also see particulars table there for data on **Argonauta**.) The fantail/elliptical counter stern is my personal favorite, and gives the boat a distinctive style and appearance all her own. Computer performance analysis verifies her fine sailing qualities, and her stability has the longest range of any that we've checked. We regard her as virtually uncapsizable.

On deck, she has a contemporary cutter rig, laid out for easy handling by her small crew. She's got plenty of sail area to make her go in light and moderate conditions, and can be quickly shortened down in a blow. The interior features private staterooms at each end of the boat. One is for the parents in the stern and one for their daughter in the bow. A variation possible is to have a double berth aft with a dresser opposite in place of the other berth, and the aft walk-in locker could become a second head.

There is a walk-through passageway from the aft cabin to the galley. Alongside this, there is a long galley counter, with an L-shape at the forward end housing the Dickinson oil range. The range is sited such that the hot side radiates heat into the cabin, making for ease of warming the crew.

Opposite the galley is a large head compartment. There is a door in the head compartment leading into the engine room, for easy access to the engine and workbench. The passageway side of the engine enclosure will also be openable for easy service. The saloon has opposing settee/berths, with a drop leaf table in between. This is open into the galley area, and will make for a roomy and pleasant social area. The deckhouse will be an operational pilothouse at sea. It will have a large workflat/chart table to starboard, over the passageway. To port, there will be a slightly lower settee and the inside control station. This settee will be raised so that the occupants will have a good view.

In the creation of the steel chine version, two sets of lines were evolved. One was a double chine version like the one done for the 45' Cat Ketch. The other was a single chine with a large radius at the chine giving much the appearance of a round-bilged boat above the water.

The interior arrangement is a slight variation on the original. A desk has been added to the main saloon, the galley range gimbaled, and the aft cabin rearranged for more locker space. Combinations of both arrangements are possible and so there are an infinite variety of others.

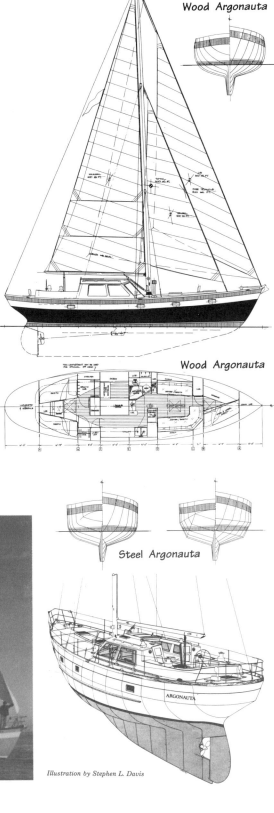

Wood Argonauta

Wood Argonauta

Steel Argonauta

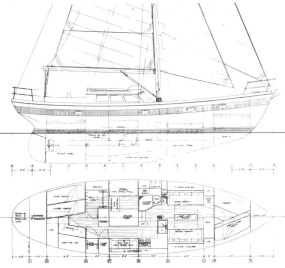

Steel Argonauta

Illustration by Stephen L. Davis

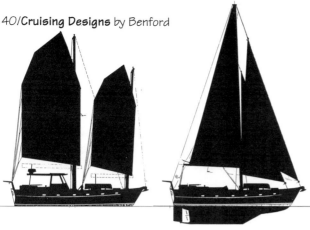

Lug Schooner Inscrutable   Inscrutable With Cutter Rig

Ketch Rigged Orphan Annie   Cutter Rigged Orphan Annie

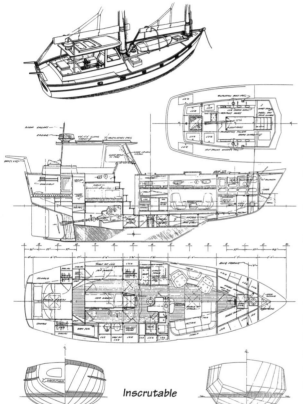

Inscrutable

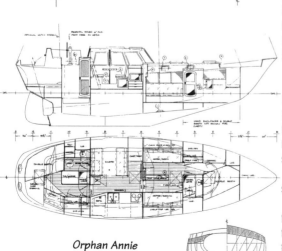

Orphan Annie

Inscrutable & Orphan Annie

45' Lug Schooner or Cutter & 45½' Cutter or Ketch
Designs Number 144 & 190
1977 & 1979

Inscrutable: The concept for this very well thought-out voyager was the result of lots of time spent voyaging on a smaller boat, dreaming of "what if" and how to do it better the next time. The clients came to us with nicely developed drawings of what they wanted, simplifying the time required to turn her out as a custom design.

The accommodations can be thought of as a three-zone living layout. The central area has the galley, navigation, head and sea berths — all in the area of least motion. The owner's cabin is in the stern and the saloon and guest cabin/workshop is in the bow.

There are two versions, the original round bilge one and the multi-chine one for steel construction. Both have good stability and sail carrying power.

Orphan Annie: These pilothouse auxiliaries are designed for multiple uses — from living aboard to passage making. They have private double staterooms with their own heads and showers at each end of the boat, giving plenty of separation for privacy with guests aboard. There is an inside and outside steering station. The outside one is in the elevated cockpit, giving great visibility forward for sailing and making landings. She has plenty of form stability to make for comfortable and powerful sailing.

Particulars:		190	144
Length overall		45'-6"	45'-6"
Length designed waterline		37'-6"	39'-0"
Beam		14'-0"	13'-11"
Draft		5'-6"	6'-0"
Freeboard:	Forward	6'-0"	6'-3"
	Least	3'-9"	4'-6 3/8"
	Aft	5'-6"	5'-5¾"
Displacement, cruising trim, lbs.		33,500	35,200
Displacement-length ratio		284	265
Ballast. lbs.		10,000	10,500
Ballast ratio		30%	30%
Sail area, sq. ft.:	Cutter	1,032	1,082
	Ketch or Schooner	1,050	1,150
Sail area-displ. ratio:	Cutter	15.88	16.12
	Ketch or Schooner	16.17	17.13
Prismatic coefficient		.54	.54
Pounds per inch immersion		1,730	1,771
Entrance half-angle		20°	22½°
Water/Fuel Tankage, Gallons		280/300	300/205
Headroom		6'-5" to 6'-7"	6'-6"
GM		4.7'	4.4'

*Caution: The displacement quoted here is for the boat in coastal cruising trim. That is, with the fuel and water tanks filled, the crew on board, as well as the crews' gear and stores in the lockers. This should not be confused with the "shipping weight" often quoted as "displacement" by some manufacturers. This should be taken into account when comparing figures and ratios between this and other designs. Also, loading down for voyaging and living aboard will add considerably to these figures, perhaps as much as 20%. Designs like these which load down gracefully and still sail well make good choices for voyaging.

46' Ketch

46' Brigantine

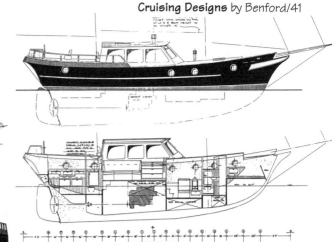

46' Ketch Toketee

Design Number 62
1970

This design is a comfortable and safe passage-maker and a great home afloat for a family. The very livable arrangement has the master cabin and head in the stern, a midships cockpit with full headroom passageway under it to the large galley, saloon, two forward cabins and head.

Designed to be a comfortable and safe passage maker while providing maximum livability for a family. Optional interior arrangements number eight to date, making for a great many alternatives to choose from!

The motorsailers are modifications of the 46' Ketch with inside and outside steering, and raised quarter deck allowing more interior space aft. Staterooms at either end of the vessel provide berths for two with enclosed head with shower, hanging locker and lounge seat. Dinette, galley and steering station with chart table is midships, and large lounging saloon is forward of midships, around a fine fireplace.

The brigantine is an optional rig for our 46' Ketch. She can be sailed as a staysail schooner without the squaresails, or with them as a brigantine. This rig can also be used with several of the different interior arrangements of the basic 46-footer, and study plans and stock plans include all these variations.

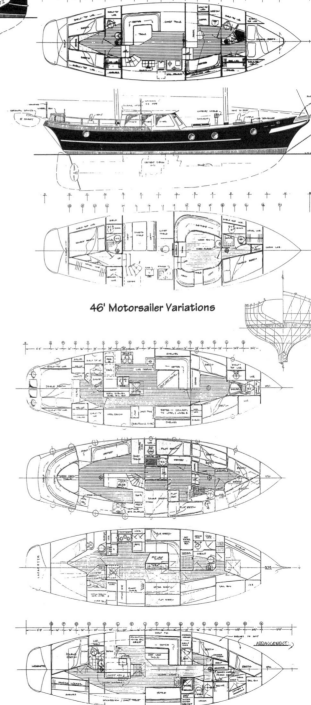

46' Motorsailer Variations

46' Ketch Variations

Particulars:		Ketch	Motorsailer	Brigantine
Length overall		46'-0"	46'-0"	46'-0"
Length designed waterline		37'-6"	37'-6"	37'-6"
Beam		13'-2"	13'-2"	13'-2"
Draft		6'-0"	6'-0"	7'-3"
Freeboard:	Forward	6'-1½"	6'-1½"	6'-1½"
	Least	3'-9"	3'-9"	3'-9"
	Aft	4'-7½"	4'-7½"	4'-7½"
Displacement, cruising trim		42,200 lbs.	42,200 lbs.	43,500 lbs.
Displacement-length ratio		357	357	368
Ballast, pounds		8,000	8,000	15,000
Ballast ratio		19%	19%	34%
Sail area, square feet		1,100	1,100	2,241
Sail area-displacement ratio		14.52	14.52	29.00
Prismatic coefficient		.579	.579	.579
Pounds per inch immersion		1,620	1,620	1,620
Entrance half-angle		23°	23°	23°
Water/Fuel Tankage, Gals.		265/140	260/300	265/140
Headroom		6'-2" to 6'-9"	6'-3" to 6'-9"	6'-2" to 6'-9"

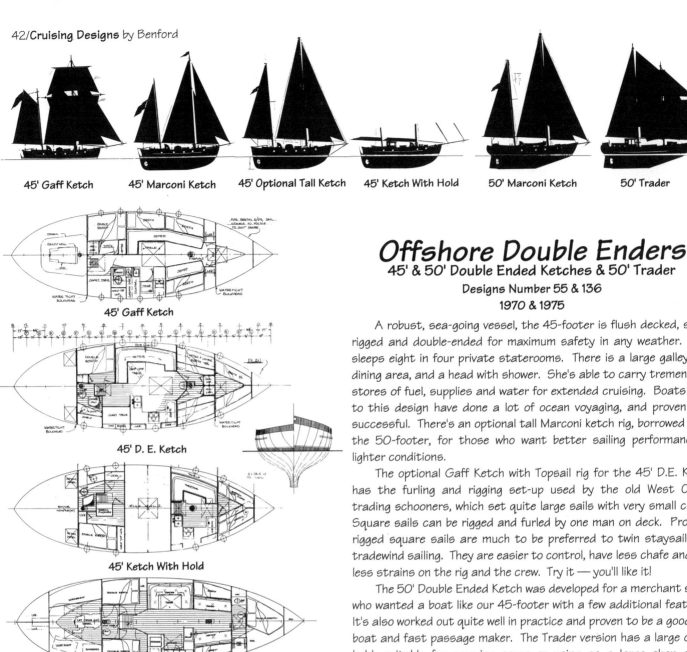

45' Gaff Ketch   45' Marconi Ketch   45' Optional Tall Ketch   45' Ketch With Hold   50' Marconi Ketch   50' Trader

45' Gaff Ketch

45' D. E. Ketch

45' Ketch With Hold

50' D. E. Ketch

50' Trader

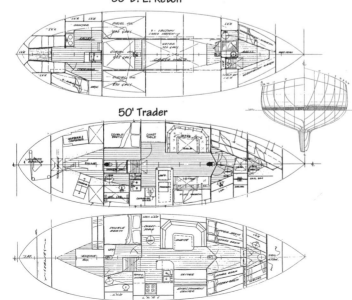

Alternate 50' Ketch Layouts

Offshore Double Enders
45' & 50' Double Ended Ketches & 50' Trader
Designs Number 55 & 136
1970 & 1975

A robust, sea-going vessel, the 45-footer is flush decked, short rigged and double-ended for maximum safety in any weather. She sleeps eight in four private staterooms. There is a large galley and dining area, and a head with shower. She's able to carry tremendous stores of fuel, supplies and water for extended cruising. Boats built to this design have done a lot of ocean voyaging, and proven very successful. There's an optional tall Marconi ketch rig, borrowed from the 50-footer, for those who want better sailing performance in lighter conditions.

The optional Gaff Ketch with Topsail rig for the 45' D.E. Ketch has the furling and rigging set-up used by the old West Coast trading schooners, which set quite large sails with very small crews. Square sails can be rigged and furled by one man on deck. Properly rigged square sails are much to be preferred to twin staysails for tradewind sailing. They are easier to control, have less chafe and put less strains on the rig and the crew. Try it — you'll like it!

The 50' Double Ended Ketch was developed for a merchant sailor who wanted a boat like our 45-footer with a few additional features. It's also worked out quite well in practice and proven to be a good sea boat and fast passage maker. The Trader version has a large cargo hold, suitable for carrying cargo or using as a large shop or as additional stateroom spaces.

Particulars:	45' D.E. Ketch	45' Gaff Ketch	50' D.E. Ketch	50' Trader
Length overall	45'-0"	45'-0"	50'-0"	50'-0"
Length designed waterline	40'-6"	40'-6"	43'-0"	43'-0"
Beam	14'-9"	14'-9"	15'-0"	15'-0"
Draft, cruising trim	6'-9"	6'-9"	7'-0"	7'-0"
Freeboard: Forward	6'-6"	6'-6"	7'-0"	7'-0"
Least	4'-0"	4'-0"	4'-0"	4'-0"
Aft	5'-0"	5'-0"	5'-6"	5'-6"
Displacement, cruising trim, lbs.	63,800 or 55,200		63,170	63,170
Displacement-length ratio	429 or 371		355	355
Ballast, pounds	18,000 to 27,000		12,500 to 19,000	
Ballast ratio	28% to 42%		20% to 30%	
Sail area, square feet	1,100	1,304	1,500	1,575
with optional or square rig	1,500	2,209		2,400
Sail area-displacement ratio	11.02	13.07	15.13	15.89
with optional or square rig	15.03	24.38		24.21
Prismatic coefficient	.562	.562	.568	.568
Pounds per inch immersion	1,950	1,950	2,343	2,343
Water/Fuel Tankage, Gallons	430/270	430/270	600/590	320/805
Headroom	6'-5" to 7'-7"		6'-1" to 7'-11"	

50' C. B. Ketch — Chanty

Design Number 63
1970

An extremely roomy 50-footer, this beamy ketch has midships cockpit with great cabin aft. She sleeps ten, including six paying guests in three private double cabins forward when used for charter work. The twin centerboards and simple Marconi rig make for easy handling, and enjoyable cruising in shallower areas such as Chesapeake Bay, Florida and the Caribbean. An exceptionally roomy vessel and versatile vessel, the plans also include some alternate interior arrangements, three of which are motorsailers.

The motorsailer (or deckhouse) version has an owners' stateroom aft, a large social area midships complete with large galley, two heads and two more staterooms forward. An excellent home afloat for a large family or several couples on long distance cruises. Two other versions with taller deckhouses are also in the plan set, and included in the study plans.

There is also a version with the quarter deck raised an extra amount. This one has an enclosed office space off the great cabin to create a private work space. It could also have an enclosed pilothouse added over the cockpit area, for there is plenty of deck space for working the ship.

An optional drawing for a seven foot draft keel version has been done, for those who would like to sail without worrying about what might happen to their centerboards. If you cruise in deeper waters, this is an alternative worth considering. Or, if you want to explore those shallower areas, take a good look at the centerboard versions. There is also a taller rig with more sail area for those wanting more performance in lighter airs.

Particulars:

Length overall		50'-0"
Length designed waterline		42'-0"
Beam		18'-0"
Draft, c.b. up or keel		4'-6" or 7'-0"
Freeboard:	Forward	7'-3"
	Least	4'-3"
	Aft	5'-6"
Displacement, cruising trim		73,500 lbs.
Displacement-length ratio		443
Sail area, square feet		1,310 to 1,530
Sail area-displacement ratio		11.95 to 13.95
Prismatic coefficient		.584
Pounds per inch immersion		2,719
Water tankage, Gals.		570 to 1,200
Fuel tankage, Gals.		584 to 1,250
Headroom		6'-6" to 6'-9"

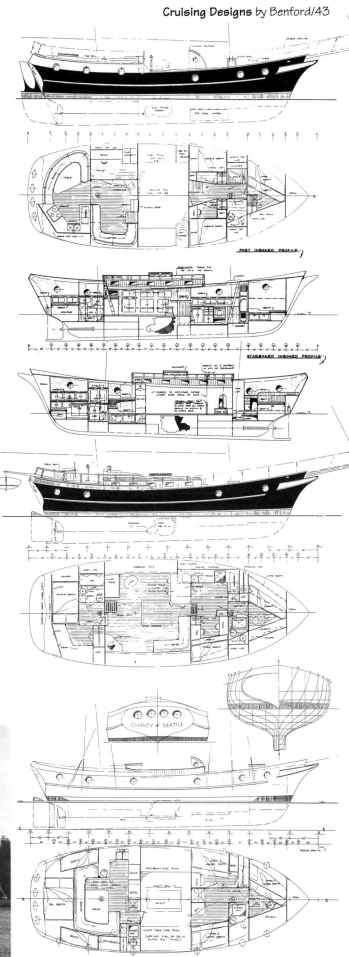

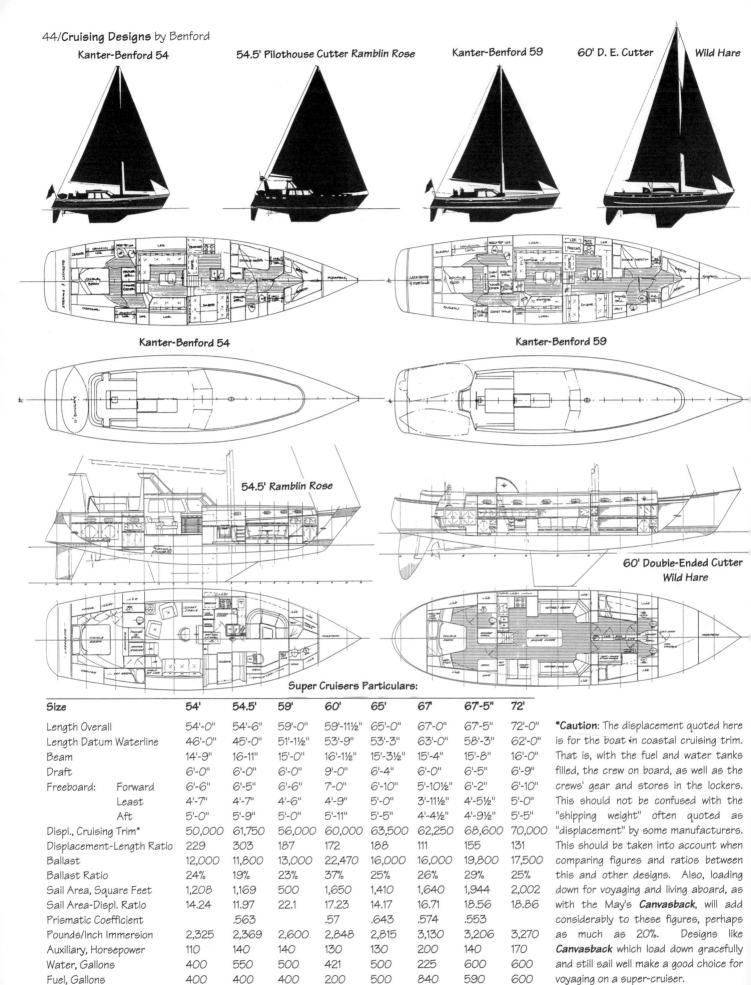

Kanter-Benford 54   54.5' Pilothouse Cutter Ramblin Rose   Kanter-Benford 59   60' D. E. Cutter   Wild Hare

Kanter-Benford 54   Kanter-Benford 59

54.5' Ramblin Rose

60' Double-Ended Cutter
Wild Hare

Super Cruisers Particulars:

Size		54'	54.5'	59'	60'	65'	67'	67-5"	72'
Length Overall		54'-0"	54'-6"	59'-0"	59'-11½"	65'-0"	67'-0"	67'-5"	72'-0"
Length Datum Waterline		46'-0"	45'-0"	51'-1½"	53'-9"	53'-3"	63'-0"	58'-3"	62'-0"
Beam		14'-9"	16-11"	15'-0"	16'-1½"	15'-3½"	15'-4"	15'-8"	16'-0"
Draft		6'-0"	6'-0"	6'-0"	9'-0"	6'-4"	6'-0"	6'-5"	6'-9"
Freeboard:	Forward	6'-6"	6'-5"	6'-6"	7'-0"	6'-10"	5'-10½"	6'-2"	6'-10"
	Least	4'-7"	4'-7"	4'-6"	4'-9"	5'-0"	3'-11½"	4'-5½"	5'-0"
	Aft	5'-0"	5'-9"	5'-0"	5'-11"	5'-5"	4'-4½"	4'-9½"	5'-5"
Displ., Cruising Trim*		50,000	61,750	56,000	60,000	63,500	62,250	68,600	70,000
Displacement-Length Ratio		229	303	187	172	188	111	155	131
Ballast		12,000	11,800	13,000	22,470	16,000	16,000	19,800	17,500
Ballast Ratio		24%	19%	23%	37%	25%	26%	29%	25%
Sail Area, Square Feet		1,208	1,169	500	1,650	1,410	1,640	1,944	2,002
Sail Area-Displ. Ratio		14.24	11.97	22.1	17.23	14.17	16.71	18.56	18.86
Prismatic Coefficient			.563		.57	.643	.574	.553	
Pounds/Inch Immersion		2,325	2,369	2,600	2,848	2,815	3,130	3,206	3,270
Auxiliary, Horsepower		110	140	140	130	130	200	140	170
Water, Gallons		400	550	500	421	500	225	600	600
Fuel, Gallons		400	400	400	200	500	840	590	600
Headroom		6'-5"	6'-6"	6'-6"	6'-10"	6'-6"	6'-5"	6'-5"	6'-6"

*Caution: The displacement quoted here is for the boat in coastal cruising trim. That is, with the fuel and water tanks filled, the crew on board, as well as the crews' gear and stores in the lockers. This should not be confused with the "shipping weight" often quoted as "displacement" by some manufacturers. This should be taken into account when comparing figures and ratios between this and other designs. Also, loading down for voyaging and living aboard, as with the May's **Canvasback**, will add considerably to these figures, perhaps as much as 20%. Designs like **Canvasback** which load down gracefully and still sail well make a good choice for voyaging on a super-cruiser.

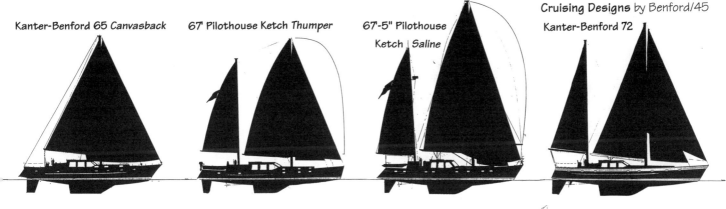

Kanter-Benford 65 Canvasback   67' Pilothouse Ketch Thumper   67'-5" Pilothouse Ketch Saline

Cruising Designs by Benford/45

Kanter-Benford 72

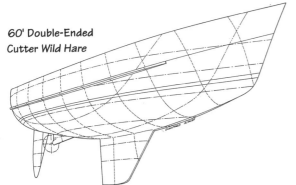

60' Double-Ended Cutter Wild Hare

Super-Cruisers

54', 54.5', 59', 60', 65', 67', 67'5" & 72' Sailing Yachts
Designs No. 279, 266, 276, 250, 249, 275, 298, 277
1988, '88, '88, '87, '86, '89, '90 & '88

These large sailing yachts are designed and outfitted to make them easy to sail with a small crew and are often handled with just a man and wife aboard. Bill May's 65-footer, *Canvasback*, was the first of this series built. She was nicely done and outfitted at Kanter Yachts and was the inspiration for the rest of this group of super-cruiser designs.

Canvasback set the theme for most of them, with a rig height that clears the 65' ICW bridges, carrying her dinghies on deck, a functional pilothouse/saloon, a good sized galley and dining area, and owner's suite aft and guest/kids quarters forward. She has a stand-up workshop/engineroom under the pilothouse.

Canvasback proved out her abilities as a passage maker, logging 1,000 miles from Florida to Bermuda in five days, motorsailing on only three days.

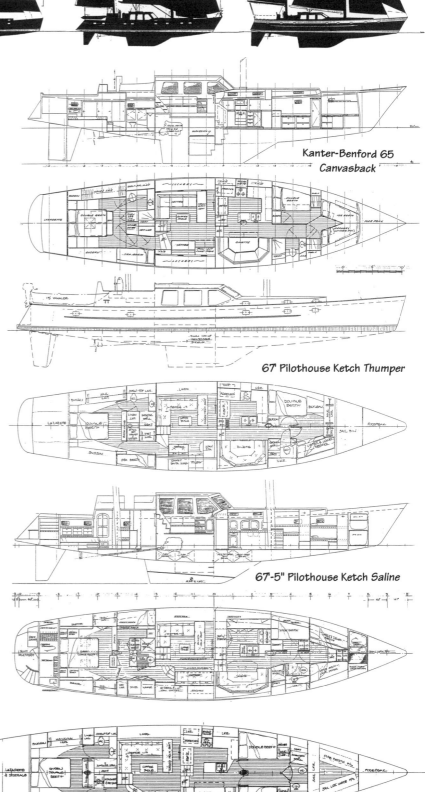

Kanter-Benford 65 Canvasback

67' Pilothouse Ketch Thumper

67'-5" Pilothouse Ketch Saline

Kanter-Benford 72

Kanter-Benford 65 Canvasback

60' Ketch Harambee

60' Topsail Schooner

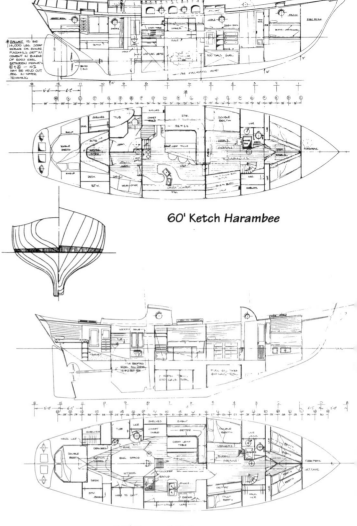

60' Ketch Harambee

60' Ketch Harambee
& 60' Topsail Schooner

Designs Number 53 & 90
1969 & 1971

Harambee has proven to be a very practical and successful charter boat. Her galley, dining and navigation areas are in the deck house. She has an easily handled wishbone ketch rig. She sleeps nine in five staterooms, has two heads, two showers, a tub, and a utility room with washer and dryer. Laid out for chartering and living aboard, she's a deluxe yacht!

The handsome 60' Topsail Schooner is a deeper keel version of the 60' Ketch hull, with a flush deck. She's designed to sleep ten in five staterooms, and will make a comfortable world cruiser. Her romantic square topsail rig could be improved by modifying it like the Great Pyramid Rig we did on the 34' *Sunrise*, which would permit all the sail handling to be done from on deck.

These larger vessels are for construction by experienced builders, for they require thousands of man-hours and a substantial amount of money to make a success of these sailing ships.

60' Topsail Schooner

Particulars:		Ketch	Schooner
Length overall		60'-0"	60'-0"
Length designed waterline		50'-0"	50'-0"
Beam		17'-9"	17'-9"
Draft		8'-0"	9'-6"
Freeboard:	Forward	7'-0"	7'-1"
	Least	3'-10"	3'-10"
	Aft	5'-0"	5'-0"
Displacement, cruising trim		100,000 lbs.	103,000 lbs.
Displacement-length ratio		357	368
Ballast		20,000 lbs.	30,000 lbs.
Ballast ratio		20%	29%
Sail area: fore and aft/total		2,150 sq. ft.	2,348/3,438 sq. ft.
Sail area-displacement ratio		15.97	17.10/25.03
Wetted surface		974 sq. ft.	996 sq. ft.
Sail area/wetted surf. ratio		2.21	2.36/3.45
Prismatic coefficient		.572	.560
Pounds per inch immersion		2,878	2,878
Entrance half-angle		22°	22°
Water tankage		800 Gals.	400 Gals.
Fuel tankage		600 Gals.	400 Gals.
Headroom		6'-0" to 7'-0"	6'-6" to 7'-8"

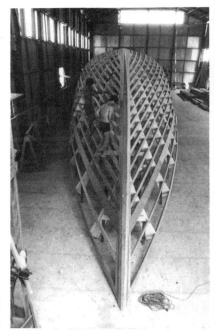

131' Ketch Antonia
Design Number 191
1980

The lovely fantail stern on **Antonia** is the aft end of the largest cold-molded sailing yacht in the world. She was built in Porto Alegre, Brazil, of Honduras Mahogany for the main structure and a variety of other native Brazilian woods for the outfitting and detailing. The workmen in the photos give an idea of the great size of this vessel.

Antonia represents a yacht only dreamed about for most sailors, and realized by the lucky few. Her spacious accommodations for the owners' party and the crew alike will make life aboard a pleasure.

A yacht of this size is capable of carrying her crew to all parts of the world in style and comfort. The graceful lines of her fantail hull allow her to be very easily driven and will be a pleasure to look at. They show that there is no upper limit to the size of a boat on which this style of elegant stern can be used. Indeed, many of the most graceful yachts and commercial vessels used to be done with fantail sterns a generation or two ago.

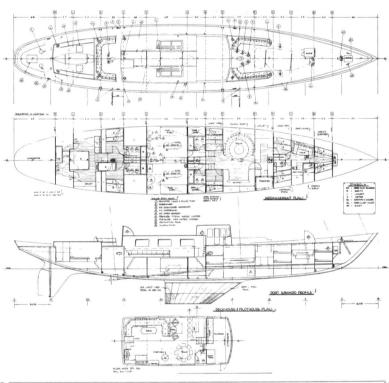

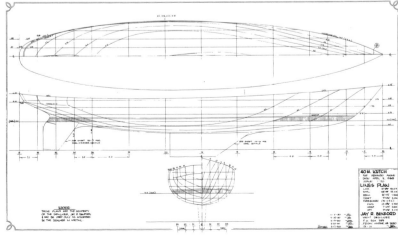

Particulars:

Length overall		131'-2¾"
Length designed waterline		108'-3¼"
Beam		24'-7¼"
Draft		12'-3 5/8"
Freeboard:	Forward	12'-3 5/8"
	Least	7'-10½"
	Aft	9'-10 1/8"
Displacement, cruising trim		228,750 lbs.
Displacement-length ratio		80.46
Ballast		65,000 lbs.
Ballast ratio		28%
Sail area		5,812.5 sq. ft.
Sail area-displacement ratio		24.86
Prismatic coefficient		.542
Pounds per inch immersion		7,253
Entrance half-angle		12°
Water tankage		4,800 Gals.
Fuel tankage		6,000 Gals.
Headroom		7'-0"

The Custom Design Process

How to do business with a yacht designer
and what is expected of the client.

Most people who have a boat custom designed have never had that experience before, and thus do not know what to expect of the naval architect and what is expected of them. In this section of the book, I will try to address these questions and define the way we, and most other yacht designers, do business. Much of the material herein is lifted straight out of our standard design contract forms with some elaboration for clarity. Since these forms were arrived at in collaboration with a number of other designers, they form a good basis for understanding the profession.

Accompanying this section are some of our preliminary designs that have yet to be completed. If one of them is either just what you like or suggests a variation that would be suitable, give us a call and we can tell you what is involved in completing the work. With finite time available to us, and the need to earn a living, we don't get to pursue all the ideas we generate.

Who Needs A Custom Design?

Fortunately, there's really no such thing as a "typical" custom design client. As all our clients are very much individuals, their differences and unique requirements are such that the most interesting and widely varying designs can be created. Perhaps some of the most pleasing clients to work with are those who have had a good deal of experience skippering a variety of boats. Such clients have selected aspects from each of their prior vessels to suit their particular, and often evolving, cruising, living, and working philosophy. In the process, they have also learned what they wish to avoid. In working with the individual custom design clients, however, the work flow most often follows a "typical" process, and the description of it here will provide a good idea of what can be expected.

The creation of a new yacht is similar in complexity of materials, equipment and form to the thousands of hours of design and engineering which go into the creation of a new airplane or automobile. A major difference arises, however, the yacht designer and his client are able to afford only a few hundred hours in developing a new design. Thus the custom yacht design client must be prepared to approach his new design on a somewhat empirical and experimental basis. The yacht designer will bring forth his best efforts, together with his many successful past experiences, to create the finest new design possible to best fit the parameters set out by the client. A client with extensive past experience in boating is the best prepared to venture into the realm of experimental ideas. For the new ideas to have the best chance of working most successfully in filling the clients' needs, they must be based on tested past experiences.

Those without experience are best off starting with used boats first. This is a much more economical way of breaking into discovering what each cruise, with its varying conditions in weather, waters, locale and crew, will reveal, to help build up a store of ideas of just what their different experiences dictate as necessary for their next vessel.

Most of the inquiries we receive deal with having a new boat custom designed, or with modifying an existing design to meet some specific need and type of service.

How To Choose A Yacht Designer

The creation of a special boat to fill a unique set of requirements can best be accomplished by those with the specialized experience, day in and day out, in doing just this. A prospective client would do well to make an overview of the market with several thoughts in mind. Firstly, which of the many designers available has created yachts which you admire or indeed love? What publications with his designs are available? With what construction materials has he accumulated extensive experience? Next, a closer inspection of this newly narrowed field should include the various designers' experiences. How successful were their yachts? Were they merely handsome in appearance and poor performers in reality? Or were their yachts of high strung performance to the detriment of the comfort and enjoyment of the rest of the boat and/or crew? Did their yacht hold together or were there problems with the construction? If the latter, was it possible to determine whether it was a builder or designer problem? (Builders have been known to make changes to the plans without letting the designer know.)

Does the designer really care about his work, or is it just another job? Often a way to tell this is what the designer does with his spare time: does he seem to enjoy cruising and/or racing (thereby accumulating more knowledge to feed into future design work) or does he spend the majority of his time elsewhere, seemingly relieved to be away from the subject? The best designers truly love their work, see it not as a 9:00 to 5:00 job, but a something they would never wish to "retire" from. Those with such an approach to the art will naturally see their job as one in which they want to do their best effort. They know that future work comes from top present performance. This includes thoughtful consultation during all stages of the boat, from design through construction and into operation of the vessel. The result: a grand yacht and a happy client.

Custom Design Procedure

The custom design process usually begins with the designer receiving a letter or phone call from the client inquiring into the possibility of creating a workable boat out of the ideas and thoughts he's collected over some period of time. From this point, letters are exchanged, or meetings arranged, to review the concept and its feasibility. The client often supplies photos and clippings of boats which appeal to him. Such details as the new vessel's intended use, desired range, speed, and rig, as well as the cruising and working philosophy of those who are to be involved in the new vessel are also discussed. Extent of design detail desired, and construction information required in the plans is also of pertinent interest. Once it's agreed that there is potential merit in the idea, the designer will explain the costs involved in the preliminary drawings.

With the payment of the retainer, the designer sets to work to give the idea some form on paper. When the designer is reasonably pleased with the drawing, two copies are sent to the client so that one can be marked with comments and questions and returned to the designer. The designer will answer the questions and give his opinions on the clients' comments, and then frequently revisions will be made to the drawings. These revised drawings will make the circuit again (sometimes more than once) until both the client and the architect are in agreement that the basic concept is well enough defined to proceed with working drawings.

Sometimes, however, the preliminaries are done as exploratory work towards seeing if an unusual idea will work, and if it is in the range of something near the projected budget. If it is not close enough to the mark, a second (or more) drawings may be made to see if the goals can be achieved by some other route. Occasionally, after the drawings are done and the quotes are in, the client decides that the boat is not what was in his mind or decides that he is unable to proceed beyond this stage. At this point, on bringing his account current for the preliminary design work, he can elect to stop the process and be under no further obligation to have the design completed.

Many times, the client will want to circulate the preliminaries for bids (also preliminary) to ascertain that the project will be within his budget. The designer usually assists in this, in recommending yards and in commenting on the bids as they are returned. Assuming the bids are reasonably close to what was expected, the next stage in the design process begins.

The evolution of the working (construction) plans and details involves perhaps the most hours of the total project, due to the extensive engineering, calculating, research, computer time, and drafting work which needs to be done. However, this part of the design usually runs more smoothly than the evolution of the preliminary conceptual work, because the gestation period has passed and the work which needs to be done — although innovative in a different way — is relatively straightforward.

However, because the design is an entirely new creation, and as such is as experimental as the previously-mentioned new plane or automobile design, there's always "fine-tuning" as the new ideas are tried and fitted into the total concept which is to be brought to life in the boat shop. The yacht designer, with fewer available hours and a much smaller staff, must depend partly on past experience, and even partly on intuition. However, the advances made in recent years in the computer industry have eliminated the need for an excessive amount of rule-of-thumb estimating. The result of the need for "fine-tuning" of a new design is that there is occasionally the need for changes while the boat is under construction. The client and the yard should be ready and able to accept this sometimes frustrating aspect of what is the natural result of working out the myriad problems inherent in bringing a brand new design to life for the first time. Naturally, the designer will make every effort to foresee as many of these problems as possible before they get to the shop, but often even the client does not realize what he has asked for, until he sees it in real life. Should he change his mind about any aspect of the design as it comes to life, this of course may affect many other parts of the vessel — all of which will need alteration accordingly, and which usually add time and cost to the project correspondingly.

As a general example, one area which can never be calculated with complete accuracy is the weights of new vessels. Even in the top production yards, which may be popping out hundreds of the same units annually, there is some variance in weights and trim between supposedly identical yachts. Each one requires

slightly different trim ballasting after launching. To exercise very great accuracy in precalculating weights of a one-off custom yacht is thus, by comparison, almost a black art. Differences between construction practices and biases from one yard to the next are difficult to prejudge on the drawing board. When the designer does know which yard is to build the yacht, he can base his estimates on weights and trim of the vessel with somewhat greater accuracy, based on his knowledge of the particular practices and prejudices of that yard.

Custom Design Fees

The fee for a custom design will vary amongst designers, depending on the extent of detail put on the drawings, the time spent on the project, and the overhead costs of the office. Some designers will charge a percentage of the cost of the construction of the boat, often in the 7 percent to 15 percent range. However, this does not always provide the most incentive for the designer to keep the cost of the boat to the client as low as he can. An alternative method is for the designer to quote a flat fee for the work, after talking over the project with the client and after reviewing the cost records from prior design jobs of similar size and complexity. The advantage of this for the client is knowing in advance the extent of the design fees. The disadvantage is that there is a strong incentive for the designer to do it as quickly as possible, making the designer reluctant to encourage improvements in the design as they occur to the parties involved, for this would entail spending unbudgeted time on the project, even though the result might be a better boat. A third method is for the designer to bill for the time spent on this job at a previously quoted rate, or rates if several staff members will be working on the job. This method leaves the designer with a clear incentive to work towards the best possible boat, knowing that the creative time spent on it will be properly reimbursed. It also allows for varying the extent of the design detail required, depending on the needs of the client and the builder. This latter method is usually our preferred method of working and we've been quite flexible in the extent of the detailing supplied, once the basics are covered and we're assured that the result will be sufficient for a good boat to result. With unusual projects, or highly sophisticated concepts for very simple boats, it is often best to approach the job on an hourly rate basis, with frequent billings so that the client can keep track of the cost of the design work on a current basis.

Delivery Time For Custom Designs

Most small jobs and revision work can be expected to take a minimum of two to three months, and may be as long as six months or more, depending on the size of the yacht. If a specific delivery time is needed to fit a construction schedule, the designer appreciates being advised of this, so that schedules can be coordinated. Most designers have a number of projects "in process" at any one time, and just getting a position on the waiting list may take additional time.

Many custom design jobs, particularly on larger yachts, can be expected to take the best part of a year to gestate smoothly from the original concept into plans for the finished yacht. It is particularly important to allow plenty of planning time during the initial, conceptual work, so that the various new ideas can have the change to be absorbed, develop further, and finally evolve into the best end product. Once the preliminary conceptual work is over, the balance of the construction drawings flow reasonably smoothly.

Construction Bid Solicitation And Review

Construction bids can be solicited from recommended yards, if desired, and review and recommendations on them provided. If this service is desired, the designer needs to know of this in advance, so that it may be included in estimating of time and expense.

Material Lists

Most designers do not normally provide separate materials lists as a part of plans for a design, as materials and equipment are already specified throughout the drawings, and the builder can generally best familiarize himself with the design by compiling a materials list as required, upon studying the plans. Should separate materials lists be desired in the plans, the client should mention this in advance, so that it may be included also in estimating of design time and expense.

Inspection

We generally inspect construction progress at the builder's site in our local travel territory. The purpose of these inspection visits is to consult with the builder, to answer any question or problems which may arise, and to generally spot-check various aspects of the vessel to see that she is coming to life in the manner which we envisaged when we originally created the plans. Some visits also cover minor changes desired by the client and/or builder, and to approve such changes so that they will not drastically affect the successful outcome of the design. It is not the intention of the designer to accept liability for the execution of construction of the vessel in accordance with every detail of in the plans, on the basis of such inspection trips, for the available time and relatively few number of visits make it impossible to accurately determine this. Rather, we rely on the builder to construct the vessel in compliance with the specifications, tolerances and materials designated in the design, so that the designed performance of the vessel can be met, and we are happy to consult with the builder in an effort to best aid him in achieving this end.

We are pleased to inspect vessels which are built outside· our generally traveled area for the cost of the travel and living expenses incurred in doing this. However, if it is a large yacht, and/or the time involved in the inspection process is considerable, then in addition, we charge for such consultation time. Quite naturally, such time subtracts from the designer's available time at the boards, but it also continues to give him/her important feedback for ongoing design

work. Each designer's policies in this area is quite different from another's.

When The Boat Is Built . . .

After launching, we enjoy, whenever possible, partaking in the builder's sea trials. Our participation thus does not end either at the drawing board or the construction site, for we take the natural extension of our interest in our work which has stimulated this new custom design, by desiring to learn exactly how she reacts to her more demanding testing grounds at sea. Taking this sort of care, we believe that we are contributing to the sort of concern and attention to detail which we expect the builder will also have brought in seeing her come to life. The result is to enhance the yacht's worth, and her future resale value. The continuing success and longevity of our firm depends on our continuing ability to create fine designs. As custom yacht design is our first love and life's work, we want to ensure the continuance of our good name by taking the time and care necessary to see our designs successfully progress from the drawing board into the water.

Reuse Of Plans

Unless otherwise specifically prearranged, building rights for one boat only are included with the design fee or purchase of a set of existing plans. All rights of design ownership remain with the designer, and the designer should be consulted for arrangements for building rights for additional vessels. The drawings and prints supplied are instruments of service and remain the property of the designer. The designer may request their return on completion of the building of the subject vessel.

Copyright

All designs, whether so marked or not, are protected by international copyright laws, and may be used and/or reproduced only with the permission of the designer. We have experienced copyright infringement in several forms. Some of these are the use of our drawings on some wrapping paper, on some business cards and stationery, on highway advertising signs, and in magazine advertisements. The great accessibility of the material makes the temptation to copy it without permission great. In most cases we would have been happy to have it used with a modest fee and/or a credit line as the source for the art. If you have the desire to use some of it just give us a call and let us come to an agreement in advance.

Expiration Of Quotes

When a designer quotes a fee for design work, quite naturally the quote would be valid for only a limited period of time. In our office, it is good for sixty days, unless otherwise stated. Thus, if a client desires to proceed with work on which a fee was quoted more than sixty days previously, it is advisable to contact us again to reaffirm the price.

Other Design Business Aspects

Beyond the creation of an entirely new design, other aspects of custom design work include modification to existing designs, consultation on other designs and/or vessels, and production design work.

Such modifications might include new interiors, new rigs, modified profiles, alternate engine-machinery, and/or alternate construction materials and methods. The basic considerations in doing such work are, to a small scale, quite similar to the creation of an entirely new design.

Consultation on such things as construction problems of any vessel, working out a new rig for an older vessel, or offering an opinion on construction method of another boat than our own design, is usually done on an hourly basis.

Production Designs

Designing for a boat which is to be built in production is another area of custom design. The basic approach is much the same as any other custom design. In addition to the process outlined earlier for proceeding with such work, the designer would also want such information as projected intentions for production quantities, construction schedules, location of construction site and intended or desired builder.

The Design Contract

The following pages have our design contract condensed without some specifics filled in. It gives an idea of what to expect when you proceed with a design. It can also be used by designers who didn't participate with the group that created it.

65' Excursion Boat

Design Number 294, 1989

The **Patriot** of St. Michaels is a 65' excursion boat, now in service in St. Michaels, Maryland, doing scenic and historic river tours for up to 210 people and dinner cruises for about 90. The **Patriot** shows another facet of our design work specializing in small ships and cruising yachts. She's built of steel, with the pilothouse and attached house built of aluminum. Her lower house has the heads, stairs, and service area all aft, with the rest of the house a wide-open space of about 940 square feet. With this versatility in adapting to different service needs she can be used for meals, dances, weddings, live music groups, or small theater productions — all in a climate controlled space.

The upper deck features a classic round front pilothouse, with an elevated bridge around it, for excellent visibility. She admeasures 50 gross tons, has fuel tankage for 2,400 gals. and water tankage for 1,300 gals.

The following drawing shows one of the things we do as a part of designing a developable hull surface, whether for steel, aluminum, plywood, or fiberglass panels. It's part of the sophisticated computer design software that we use and allows us to "unwrap" the surfaces to a flat panel.

During the design process, we use it as a check against proposed materials sizes, whether it be eight foot wide sheets of steel or plywood or some other size chosen by us or the builder. It's a real pain, let alone expense, for the builder to have to splice on a few extra inches in width to make up a panel. If we can design around the standard material sizes while it's easy to make changes either on paper or in the computer, it is a considerable savings for the builder, which can translate to profits to the builder and a reasonable price to the owner.

The process helps in the design work, allowing us to have accurate areas for doing weight calculations. Computers have certainly changed the way we do design work, and let us do more work in less time, translating into better and more accurate design work, resulting in boats that perform better and can be built in less time.

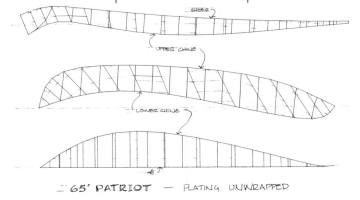

65' PATRIOT — PLATING UNWRAPPED

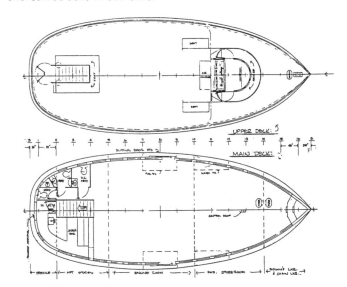

Benford Design Group

Naval Architects & Consultants
Specializing in Yacht Design

Mail: P. O. Box 447
Office: 605 Talbot Street
St. Michaels, MD 21663

Voice: 410-745-3235
Fax: 410-745-9743

(Note new area code above)

Latest revision: February 26, 1992

Design Contract

Agreement written as of the _____ day of _____ in the year of Nineteen Hundred and _____ between the **Owner** (or Client):

(Insert name and address)

and the **Architect** (or Designer):

Benford Design Group
P. O. Box 447
St. Michaels, MD 21663

For the following Project:

(Insert description of design to be created)

The Owner and the Architect agree as set forth below:

The Architect's Services consist of the elements listed below or of other elements listed as part of **Schedule B: Services & Practices.**

Article I: Preliminary Design Stage:

1) The Architect shall review the program furnished by the Owner to ascertain the requirements of the Project and shall review the understanding of such requirements with the Owner.

2) The Architect shall review, as applicable, with the Owner alternative approaches to design and construction of the Project.

3) Based on the mutually agreed upon program and Project budget requirements, the Architect shall prepare for approval by the Owner, Preliminary Design Documents including:
A) Outboard Profile sketch;
B) Accommodations sketch; and
C) Other documents as determined by the Architect to be required to illustrate the scope of the Project.

4) At the request of the Owner the Architect will submit copies of these documents to three (3) Builders of the Owner's choice for a preliminary bid estimate and assist the Owner in evaluating these estimates.

5) Compensation for the Preliminary Design Stage and any other services included as part of this fee under Article VI shall be paid as follows:

A) A fixed fee upon the execution of this agreement in the amount of _____, or

B) A retainer of _____ _____ upon execution of this agreement, with charges per the Architect's hourly rates as shown in **Schedule A: Fee Schedule** for the balance owing for the work performed.

Article II: Construction Documents Design Stage:

1) Based on the approved Preliminary Design Documents and any further adjustments in the scope of the Project by the Owner, the Architect shall prepare, for approval by the Owner, Construction Documents containing information delineated in **Article IV** setting forth in detail the requirements for the construction of the Project.

2) Prints of each drawing shall be submitted to the Owner for approval. The Owner agrees to indicate approval or disapproval within ten (10) days of receipt. If disapproved, the Owner shall promptly advise the Architect in writing of the desired changes. The Architect will revise the plans accordingly and resubmit prints for approval. Failing such notification in writing, the Architect may deem the drawings approved by the Owner. Substantial changes requested to the drawings by the Owner may be billed by the Architect based on the terms for "Additional Services" as outlined in **Schedule B**.

3) The Architect shall be the sole determiner of whether or not changes to drawings are substantial.

4) At the request of the Owner the Architect will submit copies of these documents to three (3) Builders of the Owner's choice for a construction bid estimate, and assist the Owner in evaluating these estimates.

5) The Architect agrees to perform such theoretical calculations as are customary to insure the safety and seaworthiness of the design and reasonable speed underway. The Architect will furnish a carefully prepared estimate of the speed of the vessel, but does not guarantee such speed.

6) The Architect agrees to submit the lines of the vessel to a recognized agency for model testing at the Owner's request. Observation of the tank testing by the Architect will be at the Architect's discretion or as listed in **Schedule B: Additional Services.** The Architect's presence at such test shall not be interpreted as an endorsement of the test results.

7) Compensation for the Construction Documents Design Stage and any other services included as part of this fee under **Article IV** shall be:

A) A fixed fee of _____ , payable as follows: First payment of _____ on _____, second payment of _____ on _____, third payment of _____ on _____, fourth payment of _____ on _____, and a fifth payment of _____ on completion of the drawing work. Or,

B) Hourly charges per **Schedule A: Fee Schedule** for the time spent on the Project. Billings will be submitted with each set of progress prints and the Owner will promptly pay these. (See **Schedule B** for more detail on Payments.)

Article III: Owner's Responsibilities:

1) The Owner shall provide full information regarding requirements for the Project including a program, which shall set forth the Owner's design objectives, constraints and criteria, including space requirements and relationships, vessel type and style, speed requirements, extent of equipment compliment anticipated, special equipment and systems requirements, and other general information and specifications as are pertinent to the design of the vessel.

2) If the Owner provides a budget for the Project, it shall include contingencies for bidding, changes in Work during construction, and other costs which are the responsibility of the Owner.

3) If the Owner observes or otherwise becomes aware of any fault or defect in the Project or non conformance with the Construction Documents, prompt written notice thereof shall be given by the Owner to the Architect.

4) The Owner shall furnish required information and service and shall render approvals and decisions as expeditiously as necessary for the orderly progress of the Architect's services and of the Work.

Article IV: Extent Of Agreement:

1) This Agreement represents the entire and integrated agreement between the Owner and the Architect and supersedes all prior negotiations, representations or agreements, either written or oral. This Agreement may be amended only by a written instrument signed by both Owner and Architect.

Article V: Architect Supplied Materials:

1) The information and materials to be supplied by the Architect during the Stages of the Design period are to include approximately the following lists:

The design work will be done in two Stages. The first Stage will be the Preliminary Design Phase, to define the concept of the Project. Drawings to be done include:
Preliminary Lines Plan,
Outboard Profile and/or Sail Plan,
Accommodation Plans,
Scantling Section, and
Initial Weight Study.

The second Phase, the Construction Documents Design Stage, will be to create the actual working drawings. These will include the final versions of the drawings and work done in the Preliminary Design Phase, plus:
Construction Plans and Profiles,
Inboard Profiles,
Sections of Construction Frames and Joiner and Outfitting,

Engine, Steering and Tanks, and
Deck and Rigging Plans.

Optionally, if desired or needed by the Builder, the Architect may provide:
Full Size Frame Templates on Mylar,
Plating Expansions,
Piping Schematics, and
Electrical Layout and One-line drawings.

2) The Architect may make necessary adjustments to the order in which materials are prepared or delivered based upon the Architect's determination of the most efficient design order.

3) This list is not meant to be all inclusive or to suggest that the Builder will not have to develop Shop Drawings of less significant details (which are to be submitted to the Architect for approval).

Article VI: Other Conditions Or Services:

1) It is understood that this vessel is not intended to be licensed by the U.S. Coast Guard for carrying passengers for hire.

2) (Add other specifics here)

Article VII: Attachments:

The Owner acknowledges receipt of **Schedules A, B,** and **C** which are expressly adopted and made part hereof.

(Add Owner & Architect signatures & dates)

Schedule A: Fee Schedule (effective January 1, 1992)

$/Hour   Service   (Fill in current rates)

Expert Witness
Consultation (not part of a design project)
Design Work by Jay R. Benford
Design Work by senior architect/engineer
Design Work by junior architect/engineer
Travel time by Jay R. Benford
Travel time by senior architect/engineer
Computer time running full-size frame templates
      from hulls designed on our computer facility

Computer Services to be charged as follows:

Performance Prediction of Benford design
Performance Predictions rerun with varied input

(Hydrostatics/stability studies quoted on request.)

Note: All work done under terms and conditions outlined in our standard **Design Contract** and **Schedule B: Services & Practices.** Work on all projects is started only after receipt of the retainer payment, and continued only while the account is current. Bills are due on receipt. 1.5% per month interest added to past due amounts.

Schedule B: Services & Practices

Additional Services

The following are among the Additional Services not included in the contract price unless so identified in the Design Contract. They will be provided if authorized or confirmed in writing by the Owner, and paid for by the Owner as provided in the Design Contract, in addition to the compensation for Basic Service.

1) Providing services to investigate existing conditions of a vessel or to make measured drawings thereof, or to verify the accuracy of drawings or other information furnished by the Owner.

2) To prepare or examine evaluations of the Owner's Project budget, Statements of Probable Construction Cost and Detailed Estimates of Construction Cost.

3) Submit Preliminary or Construction Documents to additional Builders, or revise Preliminary or Construction Documents to reflect changes necessary due to the Bid estimates received by the Owner.

4) Attend Tank Test, or other tests or meetings suggested by the Owner in the furtherance of the Design.

5) On-site observation visits requested by the Owner, or requested by the Builder and approved by the Owner.

6) Review of Builder's or Subcontractor's shop drawings, of Product Date, or Samples submitted by the Owner or Builder.

7) Provide additional detail drawings for the Builder, at the Owner's request.

8) Providing interior design and other similar services required for, or in connection with the selection, procurement or installation of furniture, furnishings, and other equipment, or the engineering of any unusual equipment or systems aboard. The Architect shall be the sole one to define what is regarded as unusual.

9) Making revisions in Drawings, Specifications or other documents when 1) such revisions are inconsistent with prior written authorizations, documents that have been deemed to be approved, or instructions previously given; 2) when such revisions are required by the enactment of codes, laws or regulations subsequent to the preparation of such documents, or 3) when such revisions are due to the Builder's preferences, or capabilities or other causes not solely within the control of the Architect.

10) Preparing Drawings, Specifications and supporting data and providing other services in connection with Change Orders provided such Change Orders are required by causes not solely within the control of the Architect.

11) Making investigations, surveys, valuations, inventories or detailed appraisals necessitated in connection with construction performed by the Owner.

12) Providing consultation concerning replacement of any Work damaged by fire or other cause during construction, and furnishing services as may be required in connection with the replacement of such Work.

13) Providing services made necessary by the default of the Builder, or by major defects or deficiencies in the Work of the Builder, or by failure of performance of either the Owner or Builder under the Contract for Construction.

14) Preparing a set of reproducible record drawings showing significant changes in the Work made during construction based on marked-up prints, drawings and other data furnished by the Owner and/or the Builder to the Architect.

15) Providing extensive assistance in the utilization of any equipment or system such as initial start-up or testing, adjusting and balancing, preparation of operation and maintenance manuals, training personnel for operation and maintenance, and consultation during operation.

16) Providing services to the Owner after the Architect's obligation to provide Basic Services under the Design Contract has terminated.

17) Providing any other services not otherwise included in the Design Contract or not customarily furnished in accordance with generally accepted design practice.

18) Compensation for Additional Services shall be in accordance with **Schedule A** for twelve (12) months after signing of the Design Contract. Thereafter, compensation for the Architect shall be at the then current revision to **Schedule A: Fee Schedule.**

Communications

The use of the telephone has proven to greatly speed up the design process. At the same time, we would suggest that the Client follow up all verbal authorizations or suggestions or ideas with written copies for our files. At any time, we may have a dozen or more projects in process, and while we try to keep good notes and sketches from such conversations, there is the possibility we may have missed something. Thus a fax or letter follow-up is the best insurance.

Computer Usage & Program Development

Computer rental time for equipment required beyond that owned by the Architect is billed at a rate permitting reasonable amortization of office programming expenses. Programming, including all documentation and work product is for the exclusive use of the Benford Design Group and shall be considered his property.

Construction Cost Estimating

The Benford Design Group may be asked by the Owner to make an evaluation of estimated construction costs of the completed vessel, or costs at any intermediate stage of completion. Evaluations of the Owner's project budget, statements of probable construction costs and detailed estimates of construction cost if prepared by the Architect represent the Architect's best judgment as a design professional familiar with the yacht construction industry. It is recognized, however, that neither the Architect nor the Owner has control over the cost of labor, materials or equipment, the builder's methods of determining bid prices, nor over competitive bidding, market or negotiating conditions. Accordingly, the Architect cannot and does not warrant or represent that bids or negotiated prices will not vary from the project budget proposed, established or approved by the Owner, if any, or from any statement of probable construction cost or other cost estimate or evaluation prepared by the Architect.

General Provisions

1) The Architect shall in dealings with the Builder be considered a representative of the Owner during the Vessel Construction Phase. As the Owner's agent, however, the Architect shall incur no pecuniary responsibility concerning the construction of the Project.

2) The Architect is to be furnished with written copies of all instructions supplied by the Owner to the Builder which could affect in any way the structural integrity, performance, or aesthetic value of the design.

3) On-site consultation by the Architect with the Owner and Builder may be arranged as outlined herein. The Architect shall at all times have reasonable access to the Work whenever it is in preparation or progress.

4) The Architect is to be presented with copies of all Change Orders issued which result in the modification of the vessel in any way from the original Construction Documents. No major changes, omissions, or other variations from the Construction Documents shall be made without the permission of the Architect. No such changes shall

be considered approved by the Architect unless agreed to in writing by the Architect. The Architect may bill the Owner for time spent on such items as above.

5) It is understood by the Owner that additions to or deletions of equipment or parts of the vessel as designed by the Architect will affect the handling characteristics of the completed vessel. Any such additions or deletions by the Owner or Builder are at the sole risk of the Owner, and the Architect will not be responsible for the results thereof.

6) The Architect shall perform Basic and Additional Services as expeditiously as is consistent with professional skill and care and the orderly progress of the Work. This time allocation is to be in keeping with any time constraints or commitments outlined in **Schedule C: Current Work List**.

Guarantee

A yacht compares in complexity with a car or airplane which may be the result of many hundreds of thousands of hours of design and engineering development. This contrasts with the few hundreds of hours which the Architect and his Client can afford for the designing and engineering of a new yacht. In place of exhaustive scientific and engineering research, we must sometimes depend upon past experience, rule-of-thumb calculation, and even a degree of intuition. Naturally we use our best efforts in each new design calling heavily on our years of experience designing successful vessels. Because of these complexities, however, we are simply not in a position to be able to warrant or guarantee that a new yacht will be entirely free of defects, whether caused by our error or omission, or that of the Builder.

For example, it is difficult to predict with complete accuracy the weights incorporated in a new yacht, and to visualize in three dimensions all of the spaces in a new design or the integration of a complex mechanical or electrical system. In deciding to construct a new yacht, therefore, the Owner must be prepared for the possibility that some changes may be required as work progresses or even after the yacht is completed.

Thus, the Architect is not a guarantor with respect to the results of his design. However, the Architect does commit to perform his duties in accord with the appropriate standard of care.

Insurance

Many years ago it was practical for an architect to carry "errors and omissions" insurance to protect themselves against claims arising out of potential defects in yachts constructed to their designs. Today, however, even though our record in this regard has been excellent, the cost for coverage (if available at all) is so high that having coverage is no longer feasible. As a result it is now our policy (as with most other architects) to accept a design commission only if the client agrees to:

1) Accept the risk of all defects in the yacht whether caused by the Architect's error or omission or that of the Builder.

2) Bear the cost of "errors and omissions" insurance covering our work in connection with the yacht in question.

As a result, we must expect that the client is willing to agree to release Benford Design Group and its officers, employees, and subcontractors from any and all liability, suits or causes of action arising out of, or relating to the yacht being designed.

Legal Action

Unless otherwise specified, the Design Contract shall be governed by the law of the principal place of business of the Architect. Regarding all acts or failures to act by either party, any applicable statute of limitations shall commence to run and any alleged cause of action shall

be deemed to have accrued in any and all events not later than the completion of the construction documents by the Architect.

The Architect and Owner agree that should legal action be pursued by either party, that the winning party shall be entitled to reasonable attorney's fees, in addition to other damages.

Liability

The Architect states and the Owner acknowledges that the Architect has no Professional Liability (Errors and Omissions) Insurance and is unable to reasonably obtain such insurance for claims arising out of the performance of or the failure to perform professional services, including but not limited to the preparation of reports, designs, drawings and specifications related to the design of this vessel. Accordingly, the Owner hereby agrees to bring no claim for negligence, breach of contract, or other cause of action, indemnity or otherwise against the Architect, his principals, employees, agents, sub-contractors and consultants if any claim in any way is related to the Architect's services for the design of this vessel.

The Owner further agrees to defend, indemnify and hold the Architect and his principals, employees, agents, sub-contractors and consultants harmless from any such claims that may be brought by third parties as a result of the services provided by the Architect for the Owner.

The Owner and the Architect waive all rights against each other and against the Builder, consultants, agents and employees of the other for damages covered by any liability insurance during construction. The Owner and the Architect shall require appropriate similar waivers from their Builder's consultants and agents.

Ownership of Plans

Unless otherwise agreed to by the Benford Design Group in writing the Owner is authorized to build only one vessel from the design contracted. Drawings and Specifications as instruments of service are owned by and shall remain the property of the Architect whether the Project for which they are made is executed or not. The design itself remains the exclusive property of the Benford Design Group. The Benford Design Group has the sole right to authorize subsequent use of such plans. The Owner, however, is entitled to receive complete sets of the plans developed for him.

The Owner shall be permitted to retain copies of Plans and Specifications for information and reference in connection with the Owner's use for maintenance, repair and operation of the completed vessel. Upon completion of the vessel all Plans and Specifications used by the Builder during construction shall be returned to the Architect.

(See section on **Sisterships** for information about reuse of plans and design fees due.)

Payments to the Architect

Payments for basic services, additional services, and reimbursable expenses shall be made promptly upon presentation of the Architect's statement of services rendered or expenses incurred.

Failure of the Owner to promptly pay the Architect the fees outlined in the design contract will be construed a breach of contract. In such case, the Architect has the option to continue work, suspend services until payment is rendered, or terminate the Project.

If the fees due the Architect are not paid within the time constraints permitted under the terms of the design contract, the Architect shall charge the maximum legal interest rate on all such sums from the due date until paid. If the Architect must engage a collector or an attorney to collect the fees due, the Owner shall pay reasonable collector's and/or attorney's fees whether or not legal action is instituted, and all of the Architect's collection expenses, including court costs if legal action is commenced.

If the scope of the Project or of the Architect's services is changed substantially the amounts of compensation shall be equitably adjusted.

Publicity and Marketing

The Owner agrees that the name of the Architect shall appear in all articles, information, advertisements, and brochures prepared by the Owner unless otherwise requested by the Architect. Architectural drawings appearing in such documents are to originate from the Architect or are to be approved by the Architect in writing. The Architect maintains the right to use any test data, drawings, specifications, photographs etc. of the vessel for publicity, including advertising brochures, magazine articles, etc. The Owner's name, however, may not be used by the Architect in such publicity without the Owner's express consent.

Reimbursable Expenses

Reimbursable expenses are in addition to the compensation for basic and additional services and include actual expenditures made by the Architect and the Architect's employees and consultants in the interest of the Project for the following expenses:

A) Expenses of transportation in connection with the Project (Airline tickets of over $200 will be prepaid by the Owner), living expenses in connection with out-of-town travel, and long distance telephone, fax and electronic communications.

B) Expenses of prints, reproductions, postage, small package delivery service fees and handling of drawings, specifications and other documents, excluding reproductions for the office use of the Architect and the Architect's Consultants.

C) Expenses of data processing, photographic reproduction techniques, and photographic prints.

D) Expenses of renderings, artwork, models and mock-ups, tank testing fees and expenses.

E) Expenses of overtime work requiring higher than regular rates, if authorized in advance by the Owner.

F) Expenses of any additional insurance coverage or limits, including professional liability (errors and omissions) insurance, if requested by the Owner.

Compensation for reimbursable expenses as described herein shall be computed as a multiple of one point two (1.2) times the amounts expended by the Architect and the Architect's employees and consultants in the interest of the Project.

Services

In addition to preparing preliminary plans, bidding or contract plans, and building plans, Benford Design Group may be contracted separately to perform the following functions:

A) Recommendation of bidders, circulation of requests for bids, analysis of returns, assistance of a non-legal nature to the Client or Builder, or their attorneys, in the preparation of the building contract.

B) Checking of Builder's detailed building plans, consultations with builder, preparation of addenda to specifications to embody changes approved by the Client and Builder under provisions of the construction contract, consultation on requests for extras or credits.

C) Inspection visits to the Builder's yard can be made by the Architect to observe the progress and quality of the work being performed and to note if it is proceeding in general accordance with the plans and specifications. On such visits we often check specific items

and take measurements on a sampling basis. In doing so we try to determine if defects or variation from the plans or specifications exist. We do not however supervise construction.

D) In performing such inspection visits we do not accept financial responsibility either for the cost of correcting any defect or variation from the plans or for any consequential damages caused thereby. Because we inspect only at stages of work and because of the limitations of time and of the measuring and testing facilities available to us, it is not possible for us to determine that the plans and specifications have been followed in every particular, or that details of construction and arrangement are perfect. Consequently we must rely on the Builder (and expect the Owner to rely on the Builder) to see to it that such details are properly taken care of, that the plans and specifications are followed and that defects, where they occur, are corrected.

Sisterships

The design may be licensed for serial production, by notation in the Design Contract. For this permission, the Architect will be paid a design royalty for each vessel as specified in the Design Contract. Exclusive production rights require the guarantee of a certain minimum number of royalty payments per year for the exclusivity to be in effect.

Successors and Assigns

The Owner and the Architect, respectively, bind themselves, their partners, successors, assigns and legal representatives to the other party to this agreement and to the partners, successors, assigns and legal representatives of such other party with respect to all covenants to the Design Contract. Neither the Owner nor the Architect shall assign, sublet or transfer any interest in this Design Contract without the written consent of the other.

Suspension of Project

If payments due the Architect by the Owner are not made in a timely manner in accordance with the terms of the Design Contract the Architect may at his option choose to suspend all work on the project until such payment is made. The Architect cannot be held responsible for any delays or other consequences that arise out of suspension of work resulting from either non-payment of fees by the Owner, or suspension of work requested by the Owner.

Tank Tests

Tank tests will be arranged by the Architect at the request of the Owner. The cost of these tests are billed on a time and material basis and may be expected to include tank costs, model costs, and design and analysis costs. Clients are expected to provide advance deposits to cover estimated tank billings. Tank test results, including all data and reports and the models themselves are to be considered the Architect's property and for their exclusive use.

Schedule C: Current Work List

Hull No.   Type   Scope of Project

(Add list of current projects here.)

17' Cruiser

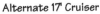
Alternate 17' Cruiser

23' Utility Boat   25' Cruiser

Alternate 17' Cruiser

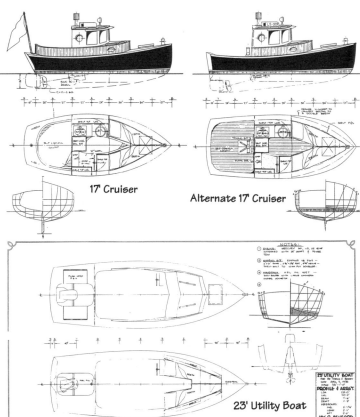
17' Cruiser   Alternate 17' Cruiser

Pocket Cruisers
Designs Number 67/119, 171 & 244
1971/1974, 1978 & 1988

17: She sleeps two, with a head and stove in her cabin. There's a comfortable 6'-3" headroom in the wheelhouse. She'll cruise at 5 knots with 5 to 10 hp diesel inboard. The alternate version will top 10 knots, with 20+ hp.

23: A planing boat, with a cuddy cabin for sleeping and getting out of the weather, plus a place for a portable toilet. She'll power easily with a medium sized outboard, or might be modified to use a stern drive or v-drive.

25: When we started this design, in 1986, we were working with a client who wanted to build it with an outboard engine for power. He'd seen our 20-footer, **Båten**, and wanted a larger version of her. While we later finished it off to use an inboard engine, I still think that she would be very practical with an outboard for power.

The inboard version was done for a fellow with a good engine in a hull that was rotting away. He decided, wisely, that it would be simpler to build a good hull and cabin that try to do a proper restoration on a dying vessel.

If I were building one, I'd want to use one of the small 4-cylinder lightweight turbo-diesels like the Yanmar JH or LH series. This would make for a much smaller engine box in the main cabin and let the galley spaces be a little bigger. It will also give performance that will surprise people who assume that this sort of styling only goes with slow boats....

The 20-foot predecessor, **Båten**, can be found in our book, **Pocket Cruisers & Tabloid Yachts, Volume 1**, with color photos and many drawings.

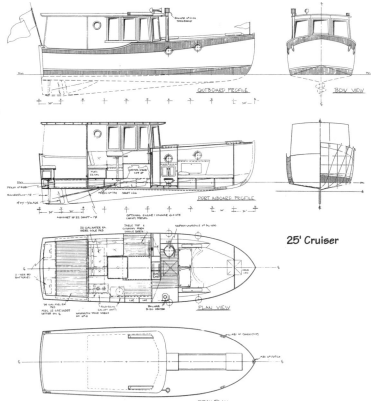
23' Utility Boat

25' Cruiser

Particulars:		17	23	25
Length Overall		17'-0"/17'-1½"	23'-0"	25'-0"
Length Designed Waterline		15'-1½"/16'-0"	20'-0"	23'-9"
Beam		7'-0"	7'-6"	7'-10"
Draft		1'-8"/2'-0"	1'-3"	2'-4½"
Freeboard:	Forward	3'-4"	3'-7¾"	4'-6"
	Least	1'-11"	2'-3"	2'-9½"
	Aft	2'-2"	2'-6"	2'-11½"
Displacement, Cruising Trim, Lbs.		2950/2920	3,335	5,000
Displacement-Length Ratio		321		
Prismatic Coefficient		.667		
Pounds Per Inch Immersion		420		
Water/Fuel Tankage, Gals.		/15		40/100
Headroom		6'-3"		6'-1½"

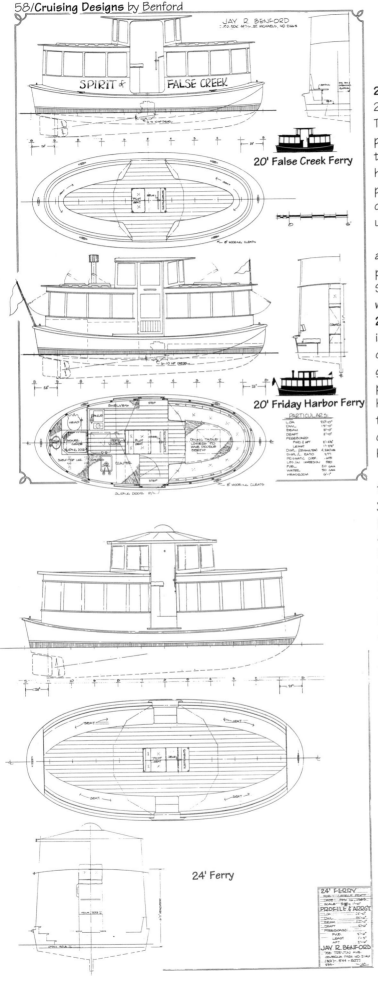

20' False Creek Ferry

20' Friday Harbor Ferry

24' Ferry

Ferry Yachts
Designs Number 212, 233 & 253
1983, 1985 & 1986

20: Paul Miller of Maple Bay, BC, has now built three fleets of the 20' ferries, which run in Vancouver and Victoria, British Columbia. They're successful workhorses, carrying their load of 12 passengers through all sorts of conditions, and carrying tremendous numbers of them. The two Vancouver fleets did heroic duty during Expo '86 there and were a big hit with the passengers. Having very low operating costs in addition to low construction costs, they are a great success. They could be used for Yacht Club shuttle or service to a private island.

The Friday Harbor version has cruising accommodations for a couple. We've lowered the cabin sole to get standing headroom, put in a galley, and provided for an enclosed head with a shower. She has all the comforts of a small motorhome, without the worry about finding a paved road to the places you want to visit.

24: The 24' Ferry was designed as an enlarged 20-footer, the idea being to double the carrying capacity of the ferry, yet operate with the same, single crew member. The extra size over gives better standing headroom and more room for the seated passengers to stretch their legs. Her power requirement is a bit higher, but the actual installed power will likely be the same since the 20s ended up overpowered in the desire to get smoother 2-cylinder engines in them. Thus, fuel consumption will be a bit higher, but probably a bit less on a per passenger-mile basis.

The 24' Friday Harbor Ferry version has all the comfortable features found on land-based motorhomes. Unlike motorhomes, you can get off the beaten path more easily and find places with privacy to anchor for the night. There are two separate sleeping areas, in the pilothouse and the convertible dinette. The roomy head has a separate tub and shower space. The galley has a refrigerator, sink, stove and storage spaces. The desk makes a nice work space for a computer, a typewriter, or doing chart work. The pilothouse is well lit and provides a commanding view for the helmsman. The raised double bed makes a good seat for daytime operations. The opening to the lower cabin can close off to make it a private stateroom at night. She makes a great liveaboard for a couple or summer home for a small family.

26: Evolved from the 24' Ferry, the 26' North Channel Ferry has a similar layout, with slightly more room due to the extra beam and length. The hull form was modified to have a more conventional bow shape to take the steeper seas expected in cruising the North Channel and going South for the winter.

Particulars:		212	233	253
Length overall		20'-0"	24'-0"	26'-0"
Length designed waterline		19'-0"	22'-6"	25'-3"
Beam		8'-0"	10'-0"	11'-2"
Draft		2'-0"	2'-6"	2'-6"
Freeboard:	Forward	2'-4½"	2'-6"	6'-3"
	Least	1'-2½"	1'-3"	0'-9"
	Aft	2'-4½"	2'-6"	3'-6"
Displacement, cruising trim, lbs.		4,260	9,000	10,000
Displacement-length ratio		277	353	277
Prismatic coefficient		.605	.598	
Pounds per inch immersion		580	859	
Water/Fuel Tankage, Gals.		50/20	132/46	
Headroom		5'-2"/6'-1"	6'-2"	6'-2"

20' False Creek Ferry

24' Ferry

24' Friday Harbor Ferry

26' North Channel Ferry

20' Friday Harbor Ferry

(Below Right) Paul Miller's shop with two of the Vancouver Aquabus fleet under construction, along with two of our Cape Scott 36' double-ended cutters. (Below Left) One of the Victoria Harbor Ferries in service. Photos courtesy of the builder.

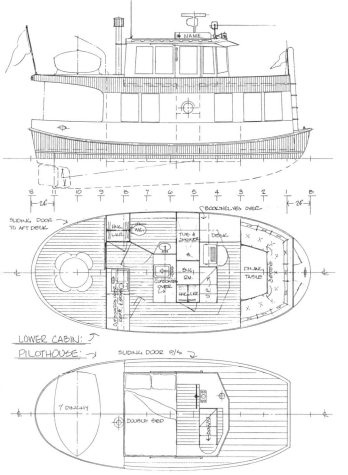

24' Friday Harbor Ferry

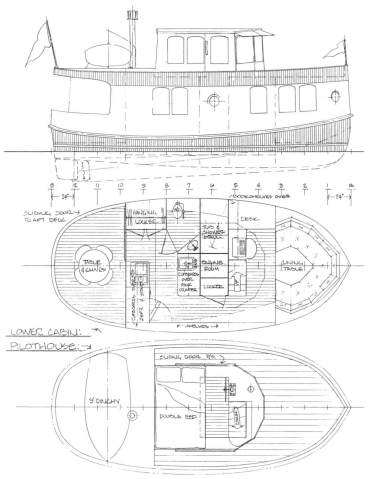

26' North Channel Ferry

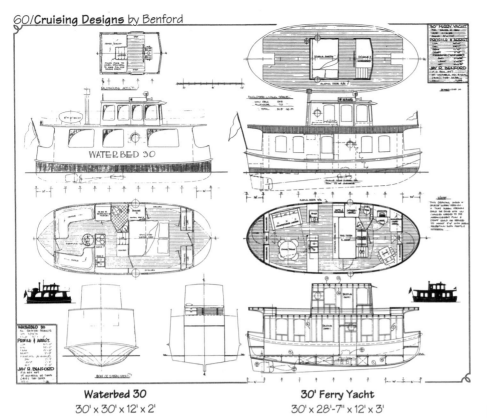

Waterbed 30
30' x 30' x 12' x 2'

30' Ferry Yacht
30' x 28'-7" x 12' x 3'

Choice Waterfront Homes

Available with panoramic marine views from Maine to Florida or Puget Sound to Alaska. An ideal liveaboard, retirement, or vacation home, the Friday Harbor Ferry offers a majestic variety of unique marine park settings, each available without ever leaving home. These luxurious homes offer low maintenance exteriors and warm wood interiors, with all utilities installed, including bathtub with shower stall, washer, and dryer. Two bedrooms, complete kitchen, large sundeck, and three viewing porches. Economical diesel power and large tankage provides for safe and low-cost operation. Neighbors too noisy? Move your house. Tired of mowing the lawn and raking leaves? Try Friday Harbor Ferry living for fast relief.

> Caution: The Sturgeon Genial warns that Friday Harbor Ferry living may be addictive and habit forming.

Ferry Yachts

Study plans for all these Ferry Yacht designs are shown in larger and greater detail in our book, SMALL SHIPS. It also has photos and more detailed information about them and scores of our other power boat designs. For more information about SMALL SHIPS, see our price list, DESIGNS & SERVICES.

These designs can be thought of as houseboats that are shaped like boats to make them socially acceptable. They have all the comforts of home — and you can take them cruising.

34' Friday Harbor Ferry
34' x 32'-9" x 13'-4" x 3'

34' Friday Harbor Ferry
34' x 32'-9" x 13'-4" x 2'-8"

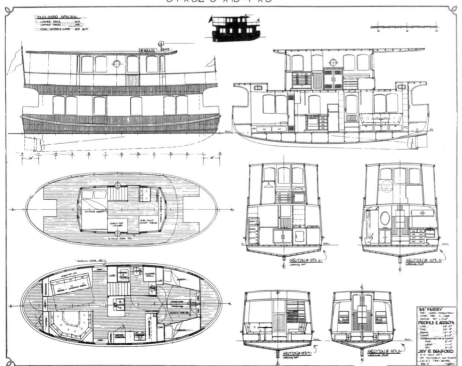

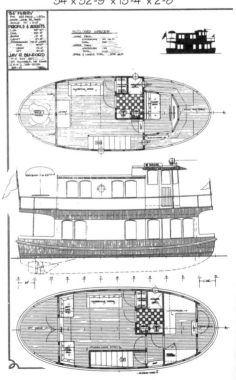

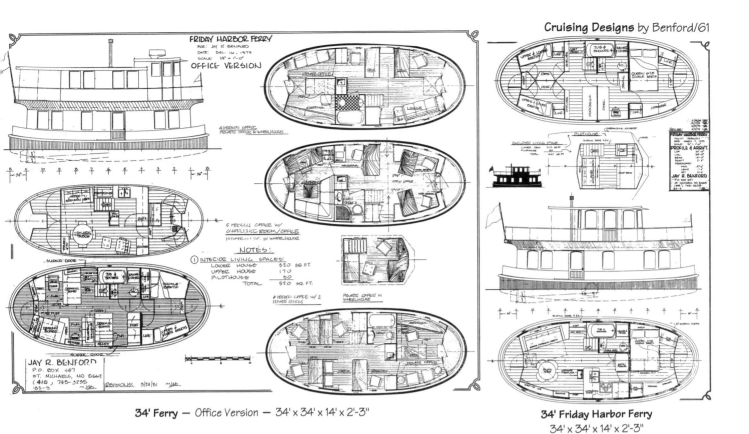

34' Ferry — Office Version — 34' x 34' x 14' x 2'-3"

34' Friday Harbor Ferry
34' x 34' x 14' x 2'-3"

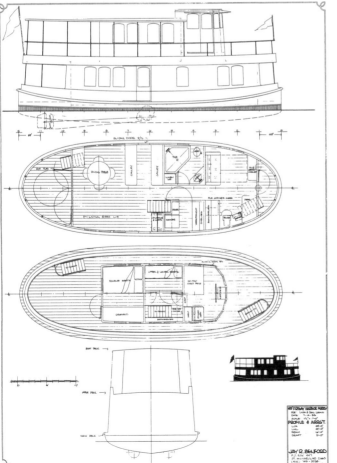

45' Friday Harbor Ferry — 45' x 45' x 16' x 3'

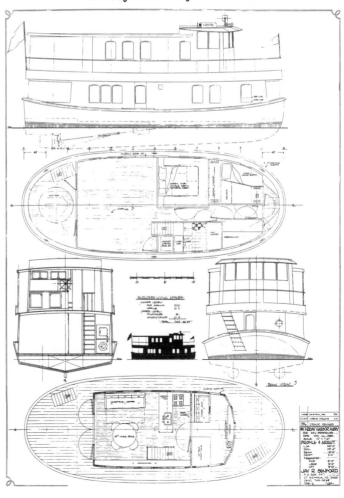

45' Friday Harbor Ferry — 45' x 44' x 18' x 3'-6"

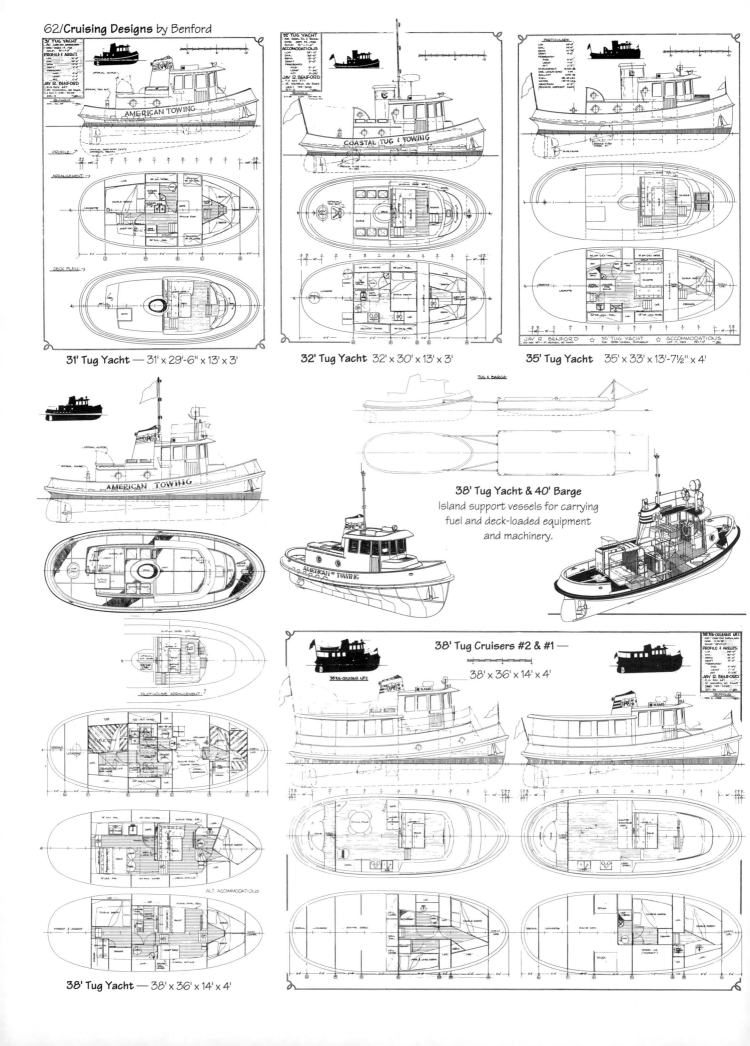

31' Tug Yacht — 31' x 29'-6" x 13' x 3'

32' Tug Yacht 32' x 30' x 13' x 3'

35' Tug Yacht 35' x 33' x 13'-7½" x 4'

38' Tug Yacht & 40' Barge

Island support vessels for carrying fuel and deck-loaded equipment and machinery.

38' Tug Cruisers #2 & #1 —

38' x 36' x 14' x 4'

38' Tug Yacht — 38' x 36' x 14' x 4'

Tug Yachts

Since I started designing working tugs almost three decades ago, I've long admired their no-nonsense salty appearance. These Tug Yachts are drawn on that heritage, keeping the true tug "look" and adding useful and practical cruising accommodations.

Study plans for all these Tug Yacht designs are shown in greater detail in our book, **Small Ships**. It also has photos and more detailed information about them and scores of our other power boat designs. For more information about **Small Ships**, see our price list, **Designs & Services**.

These tug designs can be used for work or play, serving a variety of needs. Their styling makes them appealing to both those retiring from sailing and the power boater who wants a more economical way to cruise.

"...let me say that I have spent **hours** perusing **Small Ships**...to my utter delight. Here is Benford at his best.... It's a book which will be referred to again and again."

Ted Jones, **Coastal Cruising**

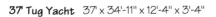
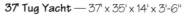

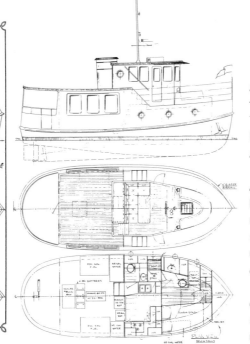

37' Tug Yacht   37' x 34'-11" x 12'-4" x 3'-4"

37' Tug Yacht — 37' x 35' x 14' x 3'-6"

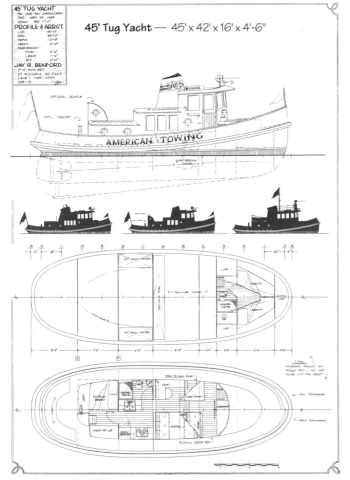

45' Tug Yacht — 45' x 42' x 16' x 4'-6"

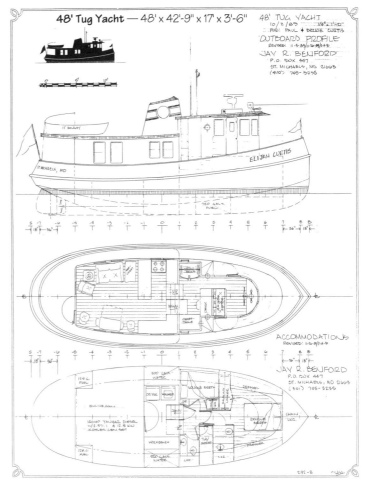

48' Tug Yacht — 48' x 42'-9" x 17' x 3'-6"

26' Trawler Yacht   **26' Deadrise Boat**   **27' Bermuda Version**   **27' Deadrise Boat**   **30' Petrel II**   **30' Deadrise Petrel**

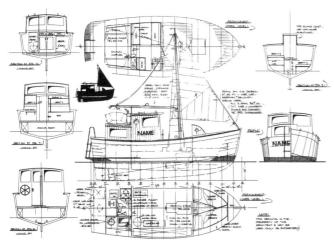

26' Trawler Yacht

Deadrise Boats

These simply built practical chine powerboats are available in a range of sizes (26', 27' & 30') and layouts. The ones shown here are a selection of the whole range.

They're inspired by the working boats on the Chesapeake Bay, with many modifications made to them as cruising boats.

They are all shown in greater detail and with more variations in our book, SMALL SHIPS. It also has photos and more detailed information about them and scores of our other power boat designs. For more information about SMALL SHIPS, see our price list, DESIGNS & SERVICES.

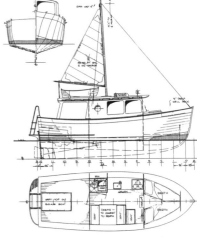

27 Deadrise Boat

30' Petrel II

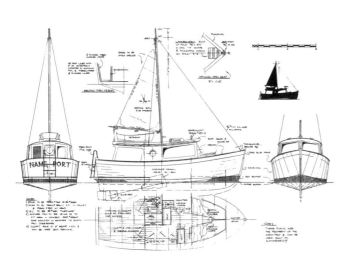

26' Deadrise Boat

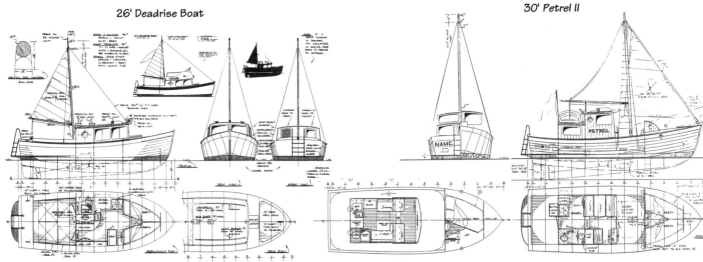

27' Bermuda Version   **30' Deadrise Boat Petrel**

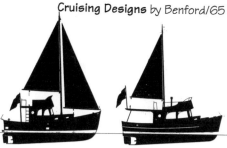

35' Strumpet

Strumpet *photo courtesy Ernest K. Gann*

32' Ladybug

32' Cruiser (#58)

32' Cruiser (#48)

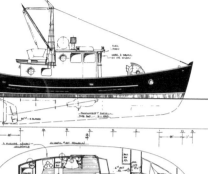

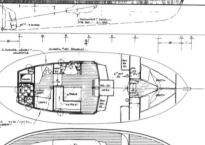

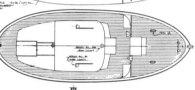

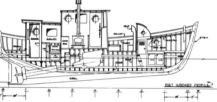

Strumpet & Ladybug

These two salty cruisers are favorites of ours. I've had a chance to be aboard both of them for periods of time, and they are great and capable cruisers. They, and a couple 32' variations, are shown on this page.

Study plans for them are shown in larger detail in our book, SMALL SHIPS. It also has more detailed information about them and scores of our other power boat designs. For more information about SMALL SHIPS, see our price list, DESIGNS & SERVICES.

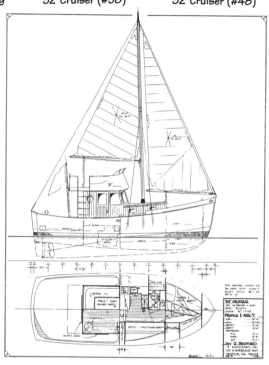

32' Cruiser (#58) *above,* **32' Ladybug** *below left,* **32' Trawler Yacht** *below center,* **32' Cruiser (#48)** *below right.*

35' Trawler Yacht Strumpet *above*

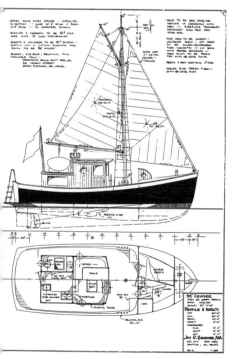

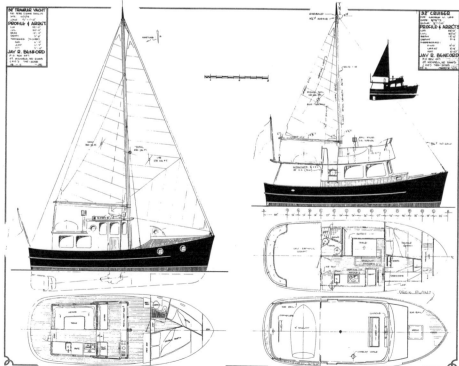

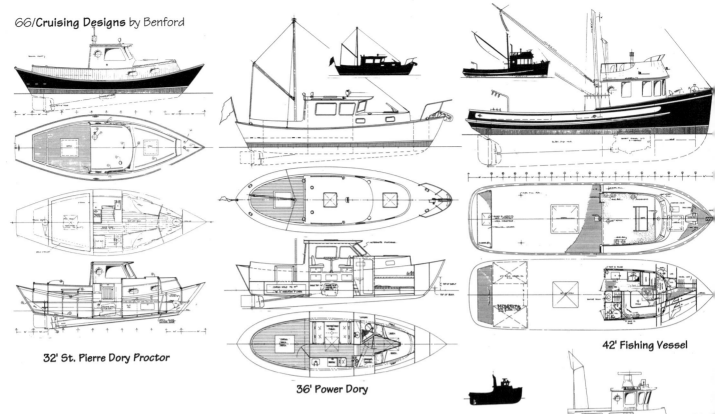

32' St. Pierre Dory Proctor

36' Power Dory

42' Fishing Vessel

Fishing Vessels

These fishing vessels are available in a range of sizes — 32', 36', 42', 46', 52' and 56'. The 32 was designed for plywood and the 36 and 56-footers for building in steel. The 36 could also be converted easily for plywood construction, like our sailing dory designs.

They are all shown in greater detail and with more variations in our book, SMALL SHIPS,. It also has photos and more detailed information about them and scores of our other power boat designs. For more information about SMALL SHIPS, see our price list, DESIGNS & SERVICES.

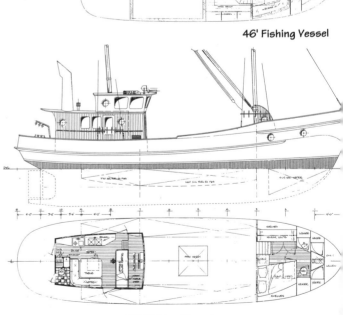

46' Fishing Vessel

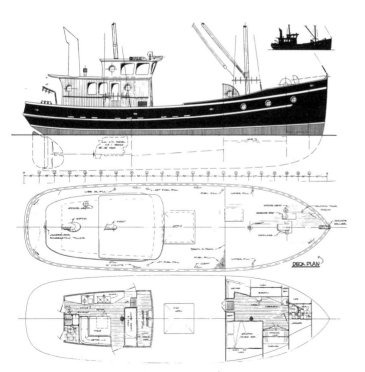

52' Fishing Vessel

56' Fishing Vessel

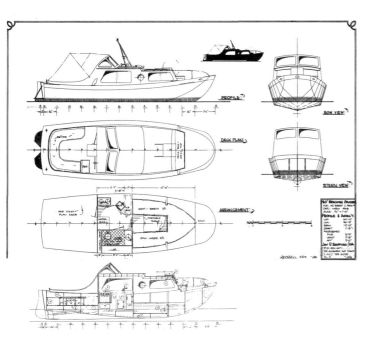

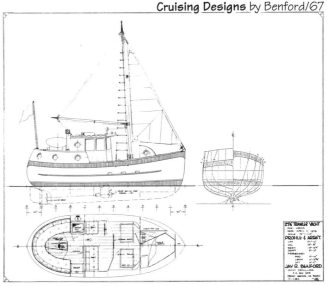

Cruisers & Trawler Yachts

The 30' Beaching Cruiser (above left) has shoal draft for cruising in thin water. Her accommodations work well for weekend or vacation use for a couple, with perhaps a couple small kids.

The 27½' Trawler Yacht (above right) would work well as a liveaboard for a young couple or a singlehander. The foc'sle has a nice double berth and there is plenty of room in the great cabin for social gatherings. Her steadying sail rig will ease the motion in a beam or following sea. There is a cargo hold area under the waist deck, for storing out-of-season clothes, extra stores, or that special piece salvaged or beachcombed on the last cruise.

The 36' Cruiser (below left) is designed for operating at semi-displacement speeds. She has a tri-cabin layout, with most of the accommodations all on one level, with only the foc'sle stateroom being down a couple of steps. (This sort of layout is increasingly popular as we get older and don't want to or can't handle a lot of climbing, yet don't want to give up cruising.) There are port and starboard recessed ladders to the boat deck, which has room for a large dinghy and plenty of seating. The flying bridge controls will be a popular place in good weather and it's extra height will be useful in making landfall in a new harbor.

The 39' Cruiser is a modification of the 36-footer, with a double chine form added to make the walkaround side decks a more useful width and a raking stem for longer length. There is also an enclosure for the forward head and a sink has been added there.

Study plans for all these trawler yacht and cruiser designs are shown in larger detail in our book, SMALL SHIPS. It also has more detailed information about them and scores of our other power boat designs. For more information about SMALL SHIPS, see our price list, DESIGNS & SERVICES.

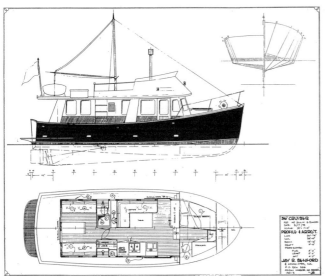

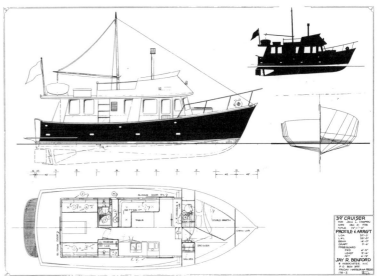

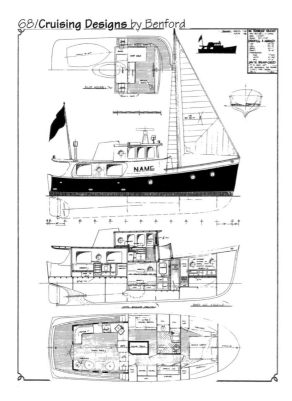

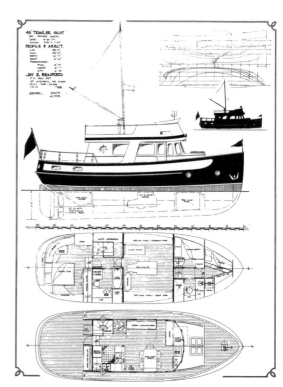

The 44' Trawler Yacht (left) is an economical long-range cruiser, with good accommodations for two to four to live aboard.

The 48' Trawler Yacht (right) evolved from the Pacific Coast fishing trollers which put to sea for long periods. She has three staterooms, with the owner's suite aft and two others forward. There is a huge engineroom and shop space. She's a great sea-going cruiser.

The 47' Motor Yacht (center) has the look of a small motorship. Designed for long-distance cruising, she would also be a comfortable home afloat, with two staterooms and heads.

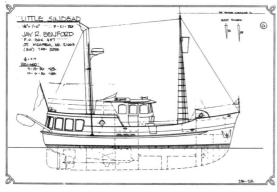

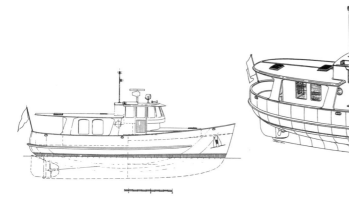

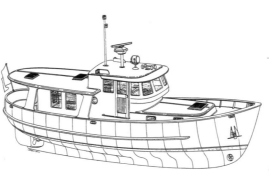

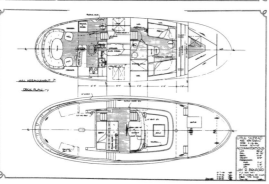

The 45' Motor Yacht, **Little Sindbad**, (left) is a small ship intended for short-handed, long-distance cruising. With a well-lit great cabin aft for her galley and dining area, she will be a comfortable vessel in which to go voyaging.

The 54' Trawler Yacht (right) is big enough to have headroom throughout her hull. This permits the passageway between the two engine rooms that connects the owner's suite aft to the forward galley and dining area and second stateroom in the bow. Note the tall stacks and the boarding platform pocketed into the stern.

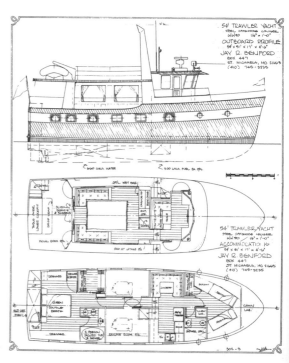

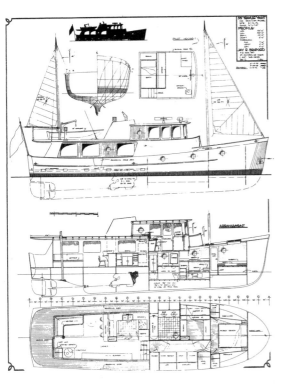

Cruisers & Trawler Yachts

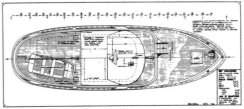

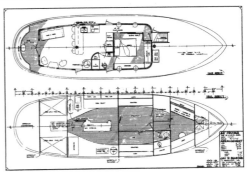

The 62' Trawler Yacht, **Indenture**, (right) has room for living aboard and to have a traveling dentist's office. This work space could be used for quite a number of other uses, too. The owner's stateroom is on deck and there's a smaller stateroom behind the pilot house. Also, the spaces in the hull could be converted for more accommodations if the office space wasn't needed.

The 55' Trawler Yacht, **Lady K**, (left) has a very roomy two stateroom layout for cruising and liveaboard use. There's an extra berth in the pilothouse for occasional use. She's very easily driven and will be economical to own and operate.

The 61' Aircraft Carrier (left) is a steel motoryacht that carries a float plane in addition to the usual small craft on the boat deck. She is laid out with the crew quarters for up to four forward, galley amidships, the saloon up behind the pilothouse, and three good sized staterooms with en suite heads aft for the owner and/or charter party.

The 65' Trawler Yacht (right) has a similar layout to the 61-footer. She too could carry something unusual on her boat deck, or you could keep it open for entertaining. Like our Freighter Yachts, she carries her small craft forward over a cargo hold space.

Study plans for all these trawler yacht and cruiser designs are shown in larger and greater detail in our book, SMALL SHIPS. It also has photos and more detailed information about them and scores of our other power boat designs. For more information about SMALL SHIPS, see our price list, DESIGNS & SERVICES.

These are but a sample of what we can create for you in the way of a distinctive and shippy motoryacht. Just the sorts of boats that will not quickly go out of style, thus proving a better long-term investment.

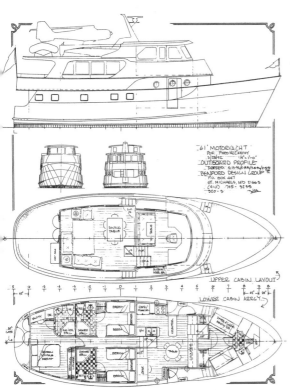

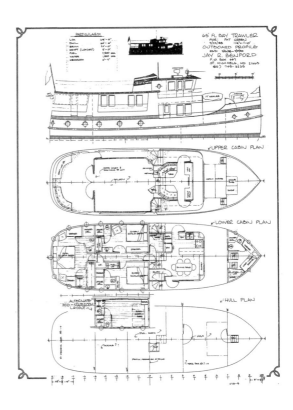

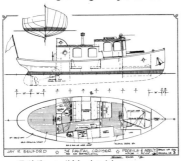

34' Fantail Yacht Memory
34' x 31' x 10'-6" x 2'-6"

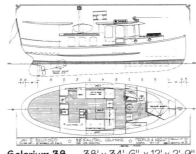

Solarium 38 — 38' x 34'-6" x 12' x 2'-9"

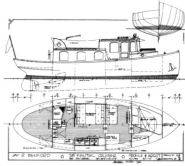

38' Fantail Yacht
38' x 34'-6" x 12' x 2'-9"

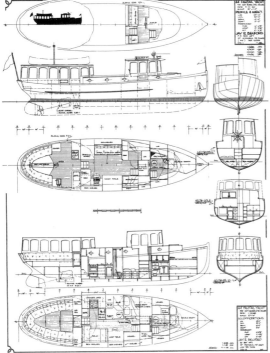

Solarium 44 Duchess — 44' x 40' x 12' x 3'

Fantail Yachts

These fantail motor yacht designs are drawn with an eye to re-creating the elegant yachts that graced our harbors a couple generations ago. They are very comfortable, economical & practical cruising boats. They will not pull water skiers or run up huge fuel bills. They **will** lend an air of sophisticated elegance good taste wherever you cruise.

Our fantail designs all take advantage of modern boatbuilding materials and the latest technology to create boats that will be long lasting and easy to live with.

Take a look at the cover photos on our **Small Ships** book to see how nicely Katy Burke (author of **The Liveaboard Book** and **Cruising Under Power**) and Taz Waller's Solarium 44, **Duchess**, turned out — distinctively different with her refined and genteel elegance.

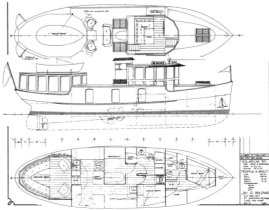

Solarium 50 — 50' x 45'-9" x 14' x 3'-6"

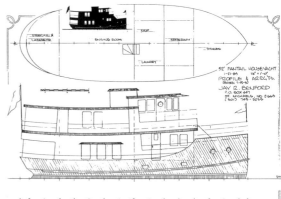

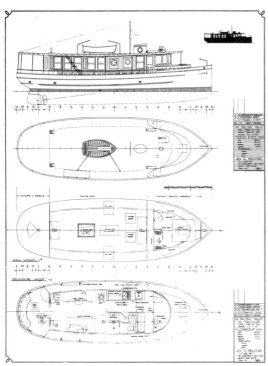

45' Fantail Yacht Tiffany — 45' x 42' x 14' x 3'

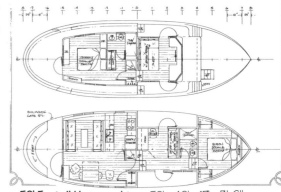

52' Fantail Houseyacht — 52' x 49' x 17' x 3'-6"

52' Fantail Motoryacht —
52' x 49' x 18' x 4'

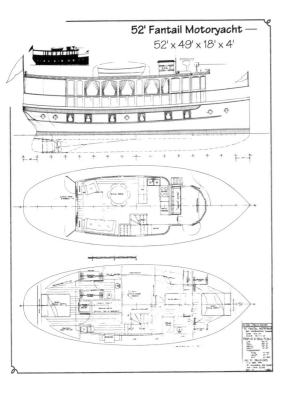

65' Fantail Yacht — 65' x 61'
x 18'-6" x 4'-6"

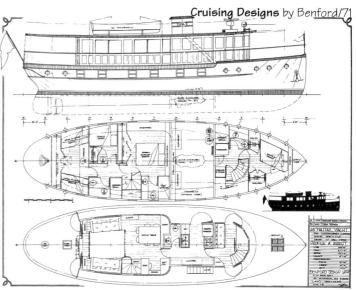

Contemporary Classics

Study plans for all these Fantail Yacht designs are shown in larger detail in our book, **SMALL SHIPS**. It also has photos and more detailed information about them and scores of our other power boat designs. For more information about **SMALL SHIPS**, see our price list, **DESIGNS & SERVICES**. Or, give us a call at 410-745-3235 to discuss how to make one of these Contemporary Classics your next yacht. Our waterways could use some more esthetic diversity and these boats will add some classic elegance.

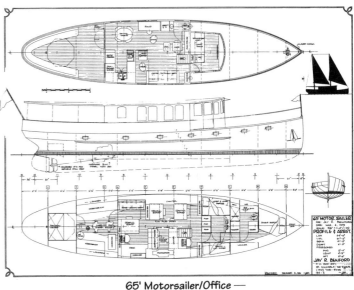

65' Motorsailer/Office —
65' x 61' x 15' x 4'

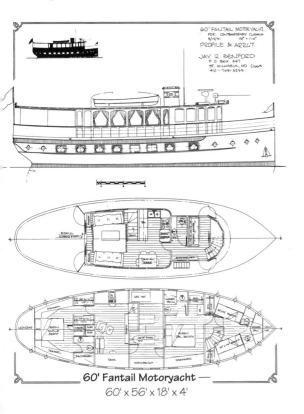

60' Fantail Motoryacht —
60' x 56' x 18' x 4'

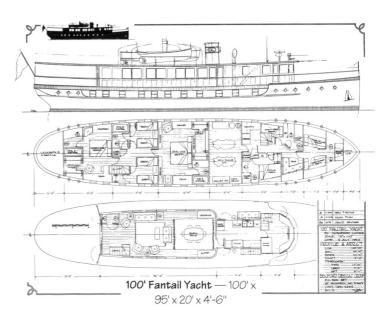

100' Fantail Yacht — 100' x
95' x 20' x 4'-6"

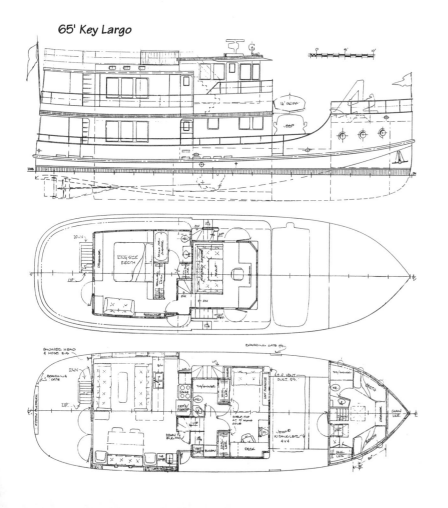

50' Florida Bay

Florida Bay Coasters

"Houses are but badly built boats so firmly aground that you cannot think of moving them.... The desire to build a house is the tired wish of a man content thenceforward with a single anchorage. The desire to build a boat is the desire of youth, unwilling yet to accept the idea of a final anchorage."

Arthur Ransome
Racundra's First Cruise, 1923

The designs on these two pages were originally done for the Florida Bay Coaster Company and licensed to them. With their company closed, we are now offering these plans to others who want to have them built.

The 50' **Florida Bay** was the first Coaster built and remains my personal favorite. I've generated a whole series of ideas on how to do a much improved version which retains all the charm and character of this practical and salty small ship.

The 65' **Key Largo** was built next, as a bigger version of the 50' **Florida Bay**, with more generous spaces throughout. She's currently in service as a charter boat, and available to anyone interested in trying out living on one of these great little ships. We've got lots of ideas for other 65-footer layouts drawn up.

The 45' **Sails** is the first of the 45' series built. They were done to provide maximized liveaboard space for people who did not need or want to carry a vehicle aboard. We've done a whole series of variation drawings on this size and their study plans are shown in our book, **Small Ships**.

65' Key Largo

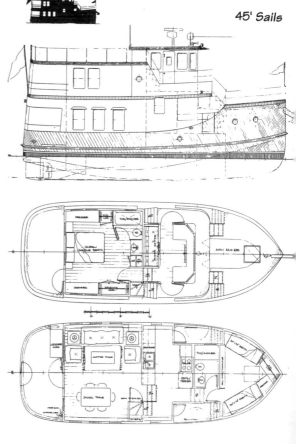

45' Sails

The 50' **Seaclusion** is the first of the revised 50' series, done as an expanded version of the successful 45's, with an extra guest cabin or study just forward of the galley.

The 55' **North Star** is like the 50' **Seaclusion** series, with extra length at both ends and substantial additions to the accommodations. She shows the extraordinary amount of living space that can be built into these ships.

Study plans for these Freighter Yachts, and many variations on them, are shown in greater detail in our book, **SMALL SHIPS**. It has photos and more detailed information about them and scores of our other power boat designs. For more information about **SMALL SHIPS**, see our price list, **DESIGNS & SERVICES**.

"...let me say that I have spent **hours** perusing **Small Ships**...to my utter delight. Here is Benford at his best with an infinite variety of arrangements and layouts on several series of working craft hulls including his Florida Bay Coaster 40, 50, and 65 footers built by Reuben Trane....

"...The varieties are endless, and if one of these doesn't start you dreaming of retiring to a life of floating luxury with your beloved, you're reading the wrong magazine....

"...original, fun, and thought provoking which is what makes this book worth owning, not just reading. It's a book which will be referred to again and again."

Ted Jones, **Coastal Cruising**

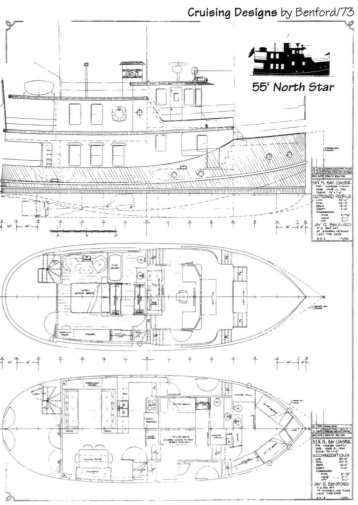

55' North Star

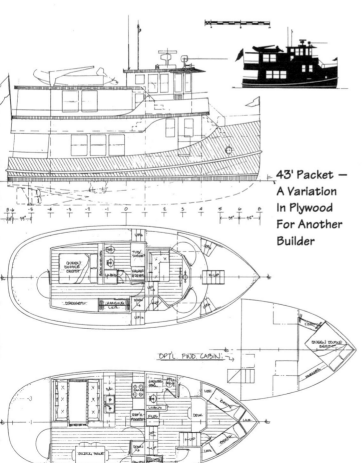

43' Packet — A Variation In Plywood For Another Builder

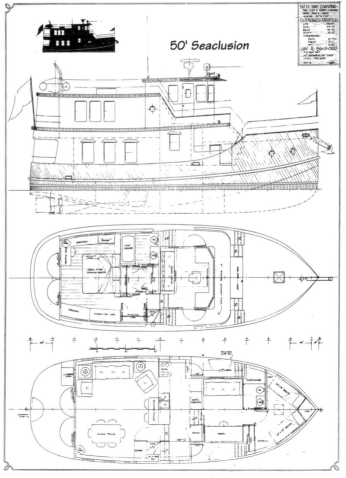

50' Seaclusion

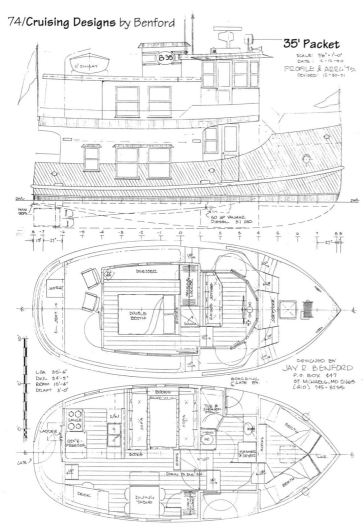

35' Packet

Design Number 300
1990

The great popularity of the Florida Bay Coasters led many people to dream of living aboard one of them. However their size and price of them made them inaccessible to many people. Knowing this problem well, we've created a solution that offers all their essentials for comfortable living aboard.

The 35' Packet is the culmination of a couple decades of relentless pursuit of one goal; the most practical and affordable home afloat. Taking our desires for a great liveaboard and combining this with over a decade's experience living aboard and about three decades of designing liveaboards, we've come up with a great boat for a summer vacation home or full time liveaboard. If you don't like the neighbors or the neighborhood, you can always move along to another area, and still be at home.

It's all here; two private bedrooms, a separate shower stall in the bathroom, a roomy kitchen with house size appliances, a dining table with real chairs, two full length sofas, good sized closets and dressers, a full sized washer and dryer, two standard twin (30" x 75") beds in the foc'sle, separate engine room, pilothouse with real glass windows at the height of most flying bridges, and plenty of porch/deck space.

The master stateroom, by virtue of it's location above the saloon, has a wonderful view of the world The windows let in lots of light and air — no claustrophobic cave dwelling here. The full sized double bed is built over drawers, and the long dresser

provides more storage. Forward is a hanging closet. Over the head of the berth are full width shelves built to fit paperbacks.

The raised pilothouse settee makes for good visibility and is long enough for stretching out on for a nap. Under the settee are drawers for storing charts and navigation information. The helmsman's position, standing at the wheel, is at the usual height for flying bridges on boats this size. But, it's got real glass in the windows for easier viewing and cleaning, and it's heated and air-conditioned for four seasons comfort.

Outside of the pilothouse, the bridgewings let the helmsman look right along either side and will greatly facilitate graceful landings. (The full 360-degree wraparound rubber fender also takes the worry out of where to hang the fenders.) From the wings, steps lead down to the foredeck or aft to the walkaround deck at the stern. This afterdeck has room for deck chairs and plenty of lounging space. Along the port side of the pilothouse is a ladder to the boatdeck. There's room for some lightweight small craft here, and a davit to lift them on and off. The stack can either house the air conditioner or be a storage locker.

Despite her apparent tall height, she has higher stability than most 50-footers. This is due to her generous beam and well designed hull form. With a loaded draft of three feet, she's a great gunkholer and the protective skeg under the prop and rudder means you just put her in reverse and power off.

The other important part about her height is that it still permits her to go up the Hudson River, through the Erie Barge Canal and out the Oswego River onto Lake Ontario. From there, West past the Niagara River to the Welland Canal and into Lake Erie and onward through the Great lakes to Chicago. There, it's through the bridges and connecting to the Mississippi River. This can lead you to side trips on the Illinois, the Ohio, and the Tenn-Tom. All this can be years of exploring the United States. Or, it can be a circumnavigation of the eastern half of the U.S.

The whole boat can be built of materials available from a good lumberyard. Good quality ply with fir framing is the basis for the whole boat. The sides of the houses are all double wall, with insulation built-in. The whole structure is glued together with epoxy, and sheathed with a skin of Dynel or 'glass cloth set in epoxy for abrasion and impact resistance. The cost of materials to build the 35' Packet is less than those for a house.

We used our Fast Yacht software to refine her hull form, providing a shape that will be easily driven with modest power. We also created a developed hull surface. The computer program

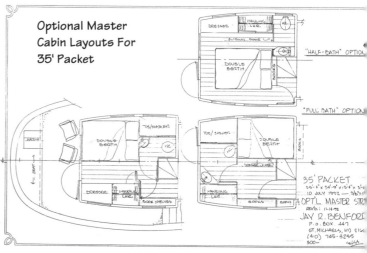

Optional Master Cabin Layouts For 35' Packet

lets us "unwrap" the panels from the hull form, and we used this part of the program early on in the design process to be sure we could get the bottom planking out of less than 8' wide sheets. (See page 51 for more on this.)

We've cut the need to use "marine" hardware and equipment wherever possible. All the kitchen, laundry, bath, heating, and air-conditioning equipment can be good quality house equipment. Even the windows and doors can be wood sash — just have 1/4" safety glass substituted for the standard 1/8" window glass.

We've designed an alternative version with a steel hull and houses, with the upper stateroom and pilothouse optionally still built in wood. This is a couple of tons heavier than the all plywood version, and has slightly larger standard tankage by virtue of having integral tanks; 300 gallons of fuel and 500 gallons of water versus 250 and 400 in the wood version. We always suggest larger water capacity in a liveaboard, since it permits longer periods of time between refills. Refilling in the middle of the winter is something to forestall as much as possible, and it's nice to have showers and do laundry on a regular basis.

Twin screw versions are certainly possible, though I'd think about a bow thruster as an alternative. Twins might let you end up with three of the same engine, if the right engines and generator were selected, thus simplifying keeping the right spares on board. I'd give serious consideration to a single screw if your normal moorage was reasonable to get in and out of, and you were willing to do a little practicing to get comfortable with your skill in handling her. The initial cost would be lower with only one engine to buy and have installed, and there would be slightly lowered fuel consumption when cruising. I admit that the extra nimbleness in maneuvering with twins has a lot of attraction, and this extra level of confidence might often mean she'd be used more frequently -- a goal worth pursuing....

How much weather can she stand, you ask? Well, probably more than any of us would intentionally set off into. And if she gets caught out in something nasty, the basic survival technique is to keep her speed down to the level at which the motion is reasonable for the circumstances. Thus, in a short, steep chop one would slow down more than in big ocean swells.

The structure is stout, her windows and doors are made to keep the water out, and her range of stability is greater than most offshore fishing vessels. My own experience in living aboard a stout offshore sailing vessel is that even those with that capable a boat will wait for good weather before making an open water crossing. It's nice to know your boat is capable of it, even if you don't feel like intentionally seeking it out.

Yes, she can be loaded on a freighter and sent to Europe to do the canals. There's only one section of the French canals that she's too big for. Or, you could send her to Seattle and cruise back and forth to Alaska, exploring the fjords of British Columbia along the way. I spent 18 years cruising out there and didn't begin to see it all. There were still areas on the Northern B.C. charts that were just outlines and no details at all.

However, for those on the East Coast, the combination of the Intra Coastal Waterway, the Great Lakes, and the Rivers systems could provide a lifetime of cruising and exploring. There are still places that are not built up, where you could settle in as a new home port, or visit on your travels. What better way to see the vastness and variety of our country? Or, use this as a way to see the sites of our history and development.

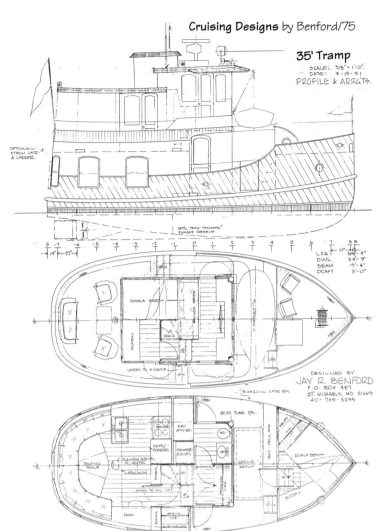

35' Tramp
SCALE: 3/8" = 1'-0"
DATE: 9-15-91
PROFILE & ARR'GTS.

DESIGNED BY:
JAY R. BENFORD
P.O. BOX 447
ST. MICHAELS, MD. 21663
410-745-3235

An alternative, for those looking for an even more "shippy" appearance, is the Tramp version, with a well deck about five feet long. The cargo hatch opens into an area below in which to stow diving gear, salvage treasures, or bicycles. The deck space can be used for lounging, carrying a personal watercraft, motorbike, or some extra fifty-five gallon drums of fuel or water.

The forward cabin shows an alternate double berth cabin layout. It can be used with the Packet also, or the Packet's twin bed version can be used on the Tramp. A four foot headroom passage could be provided through the engine room for foul/cold weather access fore and aft. The great cabin in the stern has the dining seating and the lounging seats combined around a large drop-leaf table. There is a ship's office desk opposite the galley. One thing given up in this version is the extra space for walking around the berth in the upper stateroom. We kept the aft bulkhead of the stateroom in the same location, to provide good deck space for the deck chairs. The corner posts of the pilothouse and cabin below it are tubes for the spuds. For those unfamiliar with these, spuds are weighted tubes or poles that drop through the bottom of the boat when mooring or serve as a pivot point for making a turn. These are a smaller version of those found on commercial vessels and can be equally handy to have. You could have either a power or manual winch to raise them up, with controls inside or outside the pilothouse.

For more information or prices on these small ships, call or write us at the address shown in the front of this book. The pricing is being updated as we go to press and, of course, will change with time due to the ongoing course of inflation.

Boatbuilding Materials

In this part of the book, we're taking a brief look at the various boatbuilding methods and materials. We're trying to cover each, giving the pros and cons and some opinions based on our experience. At the end there is a suggested reading list for those who want to delve further into the subjects and would like to have a starting point for their reading. Since the latest boatbuilding technology is always a moving target, some of this material will eventually be out of date. However, we like to think of our work as being mainly with "low-tech" materials and technology. We're certainly acquainted with the hi-tech world and use it for some of our work. But, use of hi-tech would not be appropriate for most of the boats in this book, not only for the expense but for the practicality of living with it and the costs of repair.

Aluminum Construction

Over the last several decades aluminum has gained in usage and acceptability. A significant portion of the custom building of larger yachts is done in aluminum, and some builders produce stock aluminum boats. This is due to the high strength to weight ratio of aluminum being attractive where speed is a prime consideration.

Great care in building is required to be sure that there are no abrupt areas in the structure. Much of this is taken into account in designing the framing and structure, but the plans must be carefully executed by the builder.

The builder must have specially trained welders to do a proper job of putting the materials together. Most of the work of cutting and drilling can be done with wood working tools.

The owner or operator must also exercise great care and caution to be sure that the boat's galvanic corrosion protection is maintained properly and that the electrical system remains isolated from the structure.

The 5000 series of aluminum alloys are normally used in marine work. They have good properties for this work and can often be left unpainted with the surface forming an oxide that protects itself from further deterioration. Of course there is no getting away from the need for antifouling paint. In this, there are specially formulated paints for use on aluminum to protect the aluminum from deterioration and slow the growth of barnacles.

If the boat is left unpainted above the waterline there will certainly be savings in maintenance costs on the coatings. However, most people paint yachts for esthetic reasons and then the coatings must be looked after. We've seen white painted topsides pick up enough yellowing at the bow in about five years that a cosmetic recoating is done. The basic paint was still in good order so the linear polyurethanes do work well.

Aluminum is a good thermal conductor. Thus all living spaces need to be well insulated to keep them dry and at comfortable temperatures. Since aluminum is quite a rigid material, care is needed to be sure that the machinery noises are well insulated and isolated from the living spaces. This means doing a good job on the isolation mounts for the machinery and sealing off any openings that can permit the transmission of airborne noise.

The majority of our past work with aluminum has been with larger sailboats that were operated with small crews. The lighter weight of the aluminum structure let them operate with smaller crews since the rigs were smaller than if the boats were built of steel. The trade-off is that the aluminum boats require more sophisticated repair facilities when and if they need work done. In powerboat design work, we would only recommend using aluminum on special use projects. For most of our cruising boats, it is hard to justify the extra expense and level of care required, both in building and in living with the boat.

We expect to see more use of aluminum in long-distance cruisers where they want to trade-off weight savings for additional fuel capacity. This is one area where it does make sense.

What About Ferro-Cement?

What Is Ferro-Cement?

For those who aren't familiar with Ferro Cement, it's a method of building in which the shell of the boat is built of a steel wire mesh and rod matrix which is permeated with a concrete mixture. The mortar is cured carefully to a minimum of 8,000 psi, to meet our specs. The resulting structure is a strong and rugged shell that will not burn, is not affected by ice, resistant to chemical attack and has a mortar that actually strengthens with age.

How Did It Get Started?

The first ferro-cement boats were built in the middle 1800's and are still in a museum in Europe. World War I saw the building of large concrete ships, some of which I've seen still afloat as breakwaters. During World War II, some experimental vessels were built which proved the material on some good sized working vessels and later on some yachts.

The building craze that began in the late 1960's was fueled mainly by promoters who spent more effort in selling franchises for their books and plans than in improving the technology. The few builders who built good quality boats often got overlooked with the vast numbers of amateur built boats sprouting up everywhere.

I had learned how to do it the right way while working for a licensee of the English Windboats Ltd. firm, who were the only ones building Lloyd's approved structures.

Following this experience, I did some additional work in the testing labs to develop a range of shell layups that would span the range of 12' to 90' designs we worked on. This knowledge gave us the technology to design much lighter and stronger boats than were commonly being done. It was an uphill battle to get people to recognize that chicken wire was not the best choice, though in the end almost everyone ended up using the same square welded mesh that we did.

Practical Ferro-Cement Boatbuilding

After a bit of this development and designing work, I teamed up and co-authored a book on the subject, titled **Practical Ferro-Cement Boatbuilding.** It was quite well received and widely distributed, going through 11,000 copies in four separate editions. This book covered the ideas, tools and techniques that we had developed to build lighter and better ferro-cement boats.

This book has been out-of-print for a long time now, though I still am able to occasionally pick up a copy in a used book store. Thus, we have a very few copies that we keep for those who are determined, usually against our advice, to build in ferro-cement.

What Ever Happened To Ferro-Cement?

Too many people who read Samson's ads saying they could build the hull and deck of a 45-footer for $2,000 didn't realize that was only the beginning of the money they would have to spend to make a complete boat. It usually took ten times that much to fully outfit the boat in those days.

Also, their publications stressed how easy and quick they were to build. Too many of the resulting boats looked like the builders took that advice literally. They were — and still are, for how do you dispose of cement? — an eyesore, enjoying very low, if any, resale value. Their being readily identifiable as ferro-cement has given a bad name to all ferro-cement boats. The good ones were always mistaken for wooden or custom fiberglass boats, and thus no credit was given to the medium of ferro-cement.

So, although it is still a viable way to build a tough and long-lasting boat, I have not been able to give it an unqualified recommendation for some time. It is very frustrating for me and much more so for the owners of the good boats to find that they can't get the same return on their invested time and money than if they had built in wood or fiberglass.

Do You Still Sell Plans For Ferro-Cement?

Yes, but only when we've given the caution above to the prospective buyers. Most of our few remaining ferro-cement sales are now going overseas where there is still a bit more viable market for the finished boats.

What About Buying A Used Ferro-Cement Boat?

With the negative attitudes prevailing about ferro-cement boats, their prices are usually quite low. The only problem in buying one is the difficulty in doing a proper survey. This is a two-part problem with the lack of many experienced surveyors and the difficulty of knowing what few clues to look for in the survey. If the seller has photos documenting the whole of the construction of the armature and the plastering, this is a big help. It they did mortar sampling and testing to assure the correct mortar strength this helps to prove the quality of the initial construction.

From there, it is a matter of looking at the level of finish and fairness of the structure, the quality of the detailing of how things are attached to the structure, and if there are any visible clues to maintenance work that has been overlooked. If you can find a good one that can be used as is and without any major investment in finishing it or adding equipment, then you might have some hope of reselling it later without loosing all your investment.

Fiberglass

Over the last several decades, fiberglass has become a sort of de facto standard for boatbuilding materials. Those of us old enough to remember its introduction recall when it was a novelty and no one knew how long it would last.

The most efficient use of fiberglass is building sister ships from a mold. There are a high number of man-hours required to get the plug, or form for the mold, truly faired and ready to lay-up the mold. Thus the best use of fiberglass is not in building one-off boats, for in building a one-off boat, it is hard to justify the expenditure of this amount of time, particularly if the boat is to be competitively priced.

Certainly the home builder can think of discounting the value of the time spent in fairing work, but the work is not pleasant and often tends to get short-changed to the detriment of the future resale value.

A one-off building technique that has been used with 'glass is the building of a large smooth table, using plastic sheet laminates (like Formica®) for the surface. On this are laid up large, flat, 'glass panels. These are then used to "plank" a hull, deck or house that has developed surfaces. The edges are trimmed and taped together and the outer gelcoated surface is repaired to make it look all alike. This method can give significant savings in labor when compared to having to manually fair all the exterior surfaces.

There are a number of core materials used with fiberglass. These serve to give insulation. They also add extra stiffness and rigidity by separating the inner and outer skins like the web of an I-beam separates the flanges for strength. Since the core is by definition sandwiched between two layers of fiberglass, it must be something that will be durable and not be subject to deterioration. Wooden cores, like end-grain balsa or plywood, can sometimes experience deterioration through water getting into them through breaks in the skin or careless installation of gear. If water does get into a wooden core, it can at best waterlog it and at worst have it all rot out and be very difficult and expensive to replace.

My preferred core materials are the closed-cell PVC foams, like Airex®, Divinycell®, Klegecell® or Termanto®, which are not subject to rotting if any water happens to get into the core. They also are good thermal insulation and can make for a surprising difference in eliminating condensation in lockers and living spaces. The techniques for installing the foam, whether in a mold or on a one-off, are well established and the material suppliers can give good guidance on how-to questions.

I have only specified closed-cell foams for core materials. These should not be confused with the cheaper foams that crumble and crush under ordinary use. Their closed-cell formulation means that water cannot migrate from one part of the foam to another and they are not subject to rotting.

The chemicals used in the resins and cleanup work are often unpleasant and need special care in handling. Some have explosive and/or toxic fumes, but there have been a lot of improvements of late and the are many more alternatives now.

The origin of the use of fiberglass in building boats is not officially known, and I would discount the stories about it being an attempt to dispose of overstocks of the foil-backed, household insulation materials....

Boatbuilding In Steel

Why Steel?

In many ways, coastal cruising is harder on the boats than offshore voyaging. This is because, as anyone who's really been cruising knows, along the coast is where boats go aground and generally bump into things. To survive this gracefully, the boat must be built of a rugged material.

Steel is an excellent material for a coastal cruiser. It is rugged. And it is easily repaired almost anywhere. Too many of the modern cruising boats are built of high tech materials, and are not repaired easily in areas with only low tech facilities. Low tech repair services are what is usually found in the out of the way places that are interesting to cruise into and where the boat might have an adventure leading to needing a repair.

Steel is typically the heaviest material used to build cruising boats. This can be used to advantage by the designer in some types of boats. The added mass of the steel can be used to design a boat that gives the comfortable motion of a much larger boat. For anyone spending periods of time coastwise cruising, most of the time ends up spent not underway, but at anchor or tied up somewhere. At these times, the higher the stability the better. The way to do this with steel boats is to keep the waterplane wide with beamy and relatively shallow boats.

The additional mass of steel over other materials means the weight of one crew member is a smaller proportion of the total displacement. Thus, moving around on the boat has less effect on her heeling and trim and thus makes for a more comfortable boat.

Although steel is probably the heaviest material, it can also be one of the most affordable, if the design is done carefully. This is because steel can be used in large pieces and assembled quickly, if the design was done for developed surface construction.

Steel boatbuilding can be done by amateurs *if* they take the time to learn welding sequencing and take care about not distorting the plating. Having a design that is thought out for ease of assembly helps make for successful construction, whether by an amateur or professional.

If the designer uses more flatbar and cut plate framing instead of flanged shapes for framing, it will be easier for the builder to do a good job of sandblasting and painting. Then, using good quality finishes, with lots of zinc in the primer coats, should give good protection. Some of our boats have been built upside-down, with the sandblasting done before rolling over, so the sand will fall out easily. This is a time-saver for the builder and is reflected in the final costs, whether these are counted in hours or dollars.

We used to join aluminum superstructures to steel hulls by stainless steel bolts in insulated sleeves, having put neoprene gasketing in between the steel and aluminum. Now, we use the explosively bonded strips of steel and aluminum, which permits welding both metals to their respective sides of the strip.

However, our usual practice is to design the whole vessel in one metal. Usually the deckhouse has lots of holes in it for the windows and hatches, and thus is not a major weight item. If the allowance for it is made in the design phase, there is no reason to go to the added expense and complication of putting an aluminum deckhouse on a steel hull.

We've been designing our structures lately to make building and outfitting as easy as we can. Sometimes this makes for a little more steel weight, but the end result is a boat that goes together quicker and saves the builder and owner money on the first cost. Some of the things we do in this vein are making the engine beds and engineroom floors all one height, so the plating or sole just lays on them, arranging for as many duplicate pieces as we can in the structure, and laying out design of the hull form and deckhouse to make maximum use of standard size plates and framing member lengths.

Insulation

My first choice for insulation is for sprayed in place foam. This is put on over the zinc-rich primer, and eliminates any pockets in which condensation might occur. The condensation that can occur behind blocks of foam stuck on the plating is the primary candidate for rusting out the steel.

If it's not possible to have sprayed on foam, then an air space all around the plating, ventilated the way a traditional wooden boat should be done, is the second choice. If this is done, I would also put a fan in the ventilation system, to slightly pressurize the bilge spaces, forcing air flow through the whole structure. I've been aboard a Dutch built 45' ketch that was over 20 years old that was built with this sort of ventilation, and she was in excellent condition. True, she needed a lot more energy expended to heat her in cool weather, but you could look at the shell plating all over, readily ascertaining it's condition.

How Long Will It Last?

Life expectancy on a steel boat can be anywhere from less than a decade to several generations. The variable in this is how well the boat is designed, built, and most importantly, how it is looked after on a regular basis. Any indications of oxidation, like visible rust bleeds and pinhole rust spotting, calls for immediate action to stop the flow of oxygen to the steel and to re-protect the surface.

Why Not Wood?

Wood is the usually my first choice in boatbuilding methods. Both of the boats that I've lived aboard, to date, have been of traditional wooden construction. They were well built and have been well maintained over the decades. As a result, they both are looking quite well, in spite of being built in 1926 and 1973. **WoodenBoat** magazine did a survey a while ago and found that boatyard operators' records indicated that cold-molded wooden boats were the best investment when all costs of ownership were considered. The warmth and charm of living with a wood boat is hard to beat, even when putting a price on it.

Carvel Planked

Carvel planking is smooth planking applied over frames that are usually steam bent in place. Sometimes there are sawn frames in some working boats or heavier cruising boats. Both of my floating homes were built of plank-on-frame construction. The major advantage of this method is the ease of replacing any particular element of the structure, if need be, at a later date.

Carvel construction, to make it weather and watertight for comfort in living aboard, requires building of top quality materials. If the materials are not well chosen and well seasoned, there could be considerable movement in the structure as the wood shrinks and swells with moisture and humidity changes. This can lead to leaks, the most annoying of which happen through the deck or cabins. If the right materials are chosen, the structure will be stable, if it is well designed and constructed. If not, there will be the frustration and possible peril of the boat leaking.

A carvel planked boat often has an inner layer of planking inside the frames, called the ceiling. (The overhead is the underside of the housetop or deck.) This ceiling provides an air passage from the bilges up to the deck. The free flow of air through here keeps the boat from growing mold and rotting out. I often advise people who are going to leave their boats for a while to put on a solar powered ventilator to pressurize the bilges to force the air flow.

Professional boatbuilders often remark that carvel construction is the quickest for them to do, which can make it the most economical to purchase.

Lapstrake or Clinker

The planking method in which the bottom edge of one plank overlaps the top edge of the next one is called either lapstrake or clinker construction. This is most often seen in small craft or dinghies, where the lightness and stiffness gained in the overlapping makes for a sturdy but light boat. It has been used for some quite large boats too, like the Viking Longships.

The skills required for this method are similar to that for carvel except the close fits have to be made on the overlaps instead of the seams that butt to each other. A popular variation on this construction now is for epoxy gluing plywood planks, which can be done in conjunction with very little inside framing. Our own 11' Oregon Peapod dinghy was built by this technique and is light and sturdy.

Strip Planking

Strip planking usually is done with planks that are almost square in cross section. They are nailed and glued together to form a rounded shape over bulkheads and mold frames. If the spans are long enough, some additional bent or sawn frames may be fitted.

Strip planking will typically support itself over longer spans than carvel planking. However, it still needs something to give it strength across the grain such as the bent frames in a carvel planked structure. One approach that has been used is to rely on heavy cloth and resin sheathing, with the strips effectively becoming a core or spacer to hold the cloth skins apart. The downside to this is that some of the poorly applied coverings sheared off the cores from lack of bonding and the differing expansion or elasticity rates of the materials. Some of this can be forestalled by putting mechanical fasteners (staples, nails, or screws) through the skins into the core.

A better alternative is to cold-mold some veneers over the strips, applying them at say opposing sixty degree angles to the strips. These would have sufficient material to take the place of the ribs and help hold the strips together. This technique would usually be my recommendation for someone building their first round bilged boat. It allows for easy handling of smaller pieces and can be done in stages.

Cold-molding

Cold-molding refers to the cold bending, as opposed to hot or steam bending, and laminating of smaller pieces and layers of wood to form the shape of the structure. As currently practiced, this is usually done with epoxy glues and sealants to stabilize the moisture content of the wood and prevent shrinking and swelling. Combined with linear polyurethane paints this produces a structure that often needs less maintenance than fiberglass, since the gelcoats need buffing and waxing and eventually need painting.

The New Zealand method of cold-molding is to set up bulkheads and temporary mold frames. Over these are bent on substantial longitudinal framing, which is let into the bulkheads and permanently fastened to the bulkheads. Then, a minimum of three layers of planking are applied on opposing forty-five degree diagonals. These are glued and fastened to the longitudinals and the bulkheads.

The combination of strip-planking with cold-molded layers over it is more often used when weight savings are not a critical issue. This results in a smooth interior which is often easier to maintain and takes less work in making sure that the pieces added during outfitting do fit well. It also means that there are no collections of bilge water on the frames since it can freely flow to the lowest point on the hull. Adding limbers to the non-watertight bulkheads and floors will facilitate using a single pickup point.

Plywood

The popularity of good epoxy glues and sealers has given plywood boatbuilding a new life. With these, the plywood can be protected from water getting into the cores and setting up rot or deterioration there. The basic principle to remember is that whenever a hole is drilled in the ply be sure that it is done a little bit over size and all the exposed edges of the ply are sealed with epoxy before installing the new piece of hardware.

The quickest wooden boatbuilding is usually using plywood in sheet form over a developed surface form. (A developed surface is one on which the plywood will lay without any distortion, such as on a cone or cylinder.) We're using our Fast Yacht computer design software to speed up the work of developing the surfaces and "unwrapping" them to check the shape and size of the panels. From this, we can be sure that we've made them in a manner that will be an economical use of the materials.

Like most strip and cold-molded boats, plywood is usually sheathed with a layer of cloth to take the local impact loads and abrasion. This sheathing is not structural on most boats, but rather a protective skin to keep harm from coming to the wood underneath.

Further Reading....

Books On Boatbuilding:

Boatbuilding by Chapelle. This books covers traditional wooden boatbuilding methods.

Boatbuilding Manual by Steward. More on wood building.

Boatbuilding With Steel by Klingel. Includes section on aluminum by Colvin.

Ferrocement by Bingham. The best of what's still in print on ferro. Excellent outfitting chapters of use with any material.

The Gougeon Brothers On Boatbuilding This is a first-rate building manual, covering using the Gougeon Brothers' WEST System™ epoxies for boatbuilding. Lots of details on how-to and techniques.

How To Build A Wooden Boat by David C. "Bud" McIntosh, illustrations by Samuel F. Manning. Good coverage on traditional wooden boatbuilding, with good and clear illustrations.

Modern Wooden Yacht Construction by John Guzzwell. A good, but hard to find, book on cold-molding by one of the real experts in the field.

Steel Boatbuilding Colvin's 2 volume set covering steel construction and outfitting.

Steelaway by Smith and Moir. A good introduction to and overview of steel boatbuilding.

Books On Design & Design Considerations:

Aero-Hydrodynamics Of Sailing by C. A. Marchaj. A sequel to the author's **Sailing Theory And Practice**. Contains a detailed study of the forces acting on a sailing yacht.

The Common Sense Of Yacht Design by L. Francis Herreshoff. Hard to find but interesting reading about the author's thoughts on the design and construction of yachts based on his lifetime of experience with some of the finest yachts and their construction.

Cruising Sailboat Kinetics, The Art, Science & Magic Of Cruising Boat Design by Danny Greene, N.A. **Cruising World** magazine's design editor explores and explains the features of cruising sailboat designs and reviews many examples.

The Design of Sailing Yachts by Pierre Gutelle. More explanations and information about how sailboats work.

Desirable and Undesirable Characteristics of Offshore Yachts By the Technical Committee of the Cruising Club of America, Edited by John Rousmaniere, illustrated by Stephen L. Davis. This book draws on the decades of experience of the contributors in exploring the features and types of boats that they've used and tried offshore.

Preliminary Design Of Boats And Ships by Cy Hamlin. An introduction to the process that designers follow to bring a new boat to life on paper and the reasoning behind the process.

The Proper Yacht, Second Edition, by Arthur Beiser. The author's philosophy explained in detail with lots of examples of suitable boats and what makes them good.

Seaworthiness, The Forgotten Factor, by C. A. Marchaj. A critique of the direction of modern racing yacht design and how this relates to a degradation in the seaworthiness of them.

Skene's Elements Of Yacht Design by Kinney. A good introduction to yacht design and the calculations involved.

Voyaging Under Power by Robert B. Beebe. Hard to find, but very useful in working through the philosophy of a power boat for long-distance cruising. Written by one who did it with lots of practical suggestions.

Other Reading:

The Boatman magazine, published in England.

Classic Boat magazine, published in England.

The Complete Live-Aboard Book by Katy Burke, with illustrations by Bruce Bingham. Good reading for anyone who may be interested in trying out this lifestyle.

Traditions and Memories of American Yachting by William P. Stephens. An excellent history of the sport up through the W.W.II era. New 50th anniversary edition is expanded in its coverage and easy to read.

Voyaging On A Small Income by Annie Hill. Very interesting first-hand look into the philosophy and life of the career voyager, by someone who is doing it full time (aboard one of our 34' sailing dory designs).

WoodenBoat, An Appreciation of the Craft by the Editors of **WoodenBoat** Magazine. A selection of the best from the articles in the magazine.

WoodenBoat magazine, published in Maine.

A Caution....

Just as the foregoing pages contain my opinions, prejudices and experiences, you will find the same is true in the pages of these other books. In the end, you will have to weigh all the evidence and make a decision on what materials to use based on your skills and what materials are available to you to use. We wish you well and would look forward to the opportunity to create a boat together.

25' Tug Yacht

Design number 325
1994

The design brief for this boat was to create a vessel that would be useful for overnighting and day cruises on a lake in Switzerland. The pilothouse has two raised seats for the Skipper and Mate to see where they're going. Down a couple steps forward are the head and sink, in an area that can be separated for privacy from the rest of the boat. The main cabin has two settee berths for sitting inside out of the weather. The center section forward of them has a piece that pulls aft and makes them into a wide double berth. The galley is across the after end of this saloon. The icebox has two hatches for access from in the saloon and out in the cockpit. The optional canopy over the aft deck will provide both sun and rain shelter.

The 25' Tug plans are in Metric scales (mostly 1:20) and well detailed, including a set of computer faired and drawn patterns for the frames, shown small scale below. Plating panel "unwraps" are also part of the plan package. Construction of the single chine hull form (with developable surfaces) is robust with conservative steel scantlings. She has integral tankage for both fuel and water. Power is a Yanmar 27hp diesel — more than enough to drive her to hull speed and just right for very economical operation.

This type of design could readily be converted to build in plywood and epoxy or panel fiberglass or aluminum. If you're interested in seeing about having it converted, call and ask us to quote you on the revision work. She's a salty cruiser and would be lots of fun to build and cruise.

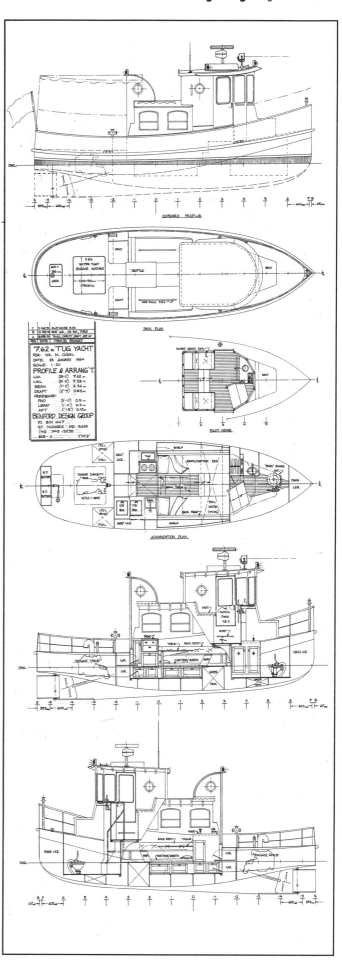

Particulars:

Length overall	25'-0"
Length designed waterline	24'-10"
Beam	7'-9"
Draft	2'-9"
Freeboard:	
Forward	3'-0"
Least	1'-0"
Aft	1'-5"
Displacement, cruising trim	10,000 lbs
Displacement-length ratio	290
Prismatic coefficient	.564
Water tankage	103 Gal.
Fuel tankage	90 Gal.
Headroom	6'-8"

*CAUTION: The displacement quoted here is for the boat in cruising trim. That is, with the fuel and water tanks filled, the crew on board, as well as the crews' gear and store in the locker. This should not be confused with the "shipping weight" often quoted as "displacement" by some manufacturers. This should be taken into account when comparing figures and ratios between this and other designs.

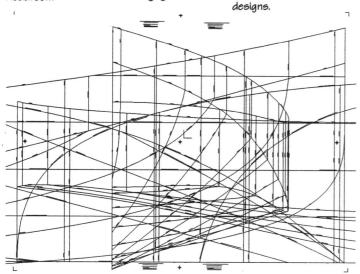

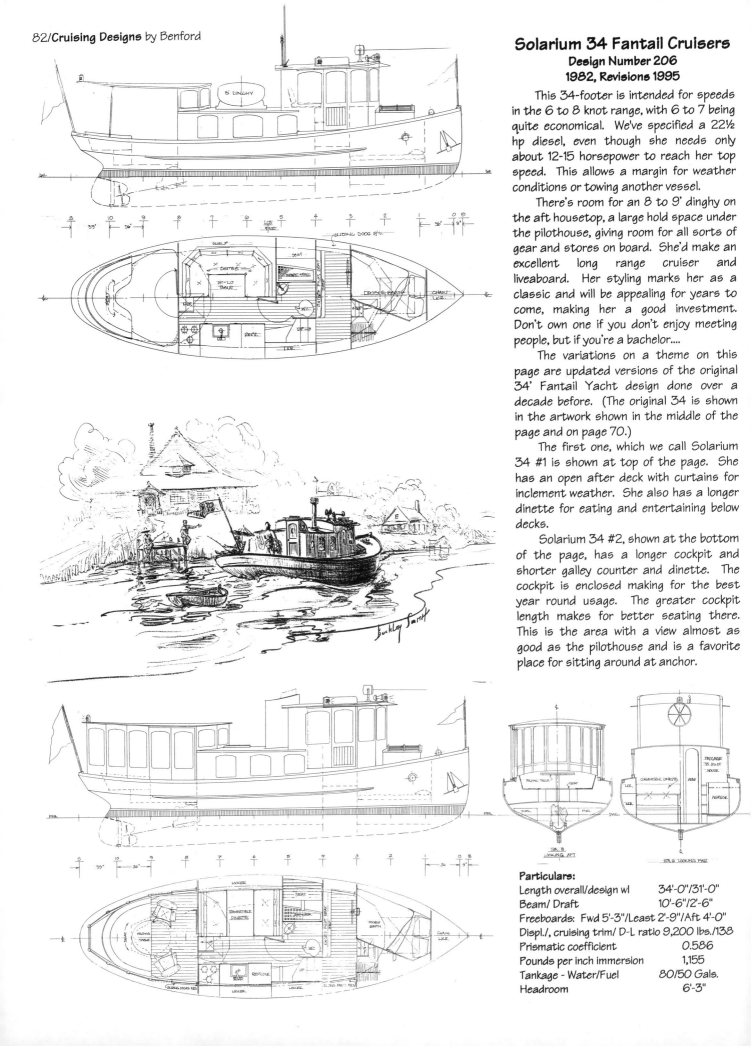

Solarium 34 Fantail Cruisers
Design Number 206
1982, Revisions 1995

This 34-footer is intended for speeds in the 6 to 8 knot range, with 6 to 7 being quite economical. We've specified a 22½ hp diesel, even though she needs only about 12-15 horsepower to reach her top speed. This allows a margin for weather conditions or towing another vessel.

There's room for an 8 to 9' dinghy on the aft housetop, a large hold space under the pilothouse, giving room for all sorts of gear and stores on board. She'd make an excellent long range cruiser and liveaboard. Her styling marks her as a classic and will be appealing for years to come, making her a good investment. Don't own one if you don't enjoy meeting people, but if you're a bachelor....

The variations on a theme on this page are updated versions of the original 34' Fantail Yacht design done over a decade before. (The original 34 is shown in the artwork shown in the middle of the page and on page 70.)

The first one, which we call Solarium 34 #1 is shown at top of the page. She has an open after deck with curtains for inclement weather. She also has a longer dinette for eating and entertaining below decks.

Solarium 34 #2, shown at the bottom of the page, has a longer cockpit and shorter galley counter and dinette. The cockpit is enclosed making for the best year round usage. The greater cockpit length makes for better seating there. This is the area with a view almost as good as the pilothouse and is a favorite place for sitting around at anchor.

Particulars:

Length overall/design wl	34'-0"/31'-0"
Beam/ Draft	10'-6"/2'-6"
Freeboards: Fwd 5'-3"/Least 2'-9"/Aft 4'-0"	
Displ./, cruising trim/ D-L ratio 9,200 lbs./138	
Prismatic coefficient	0.586
Pounds per inch immersion	1,155
Tankage - Water/Fuel	80/50 Gals.
Headroom	6'-3"

35' Trawler

Design Number 300
1994

This trawler yacht is an evolutionary development based on our 35' Packet design, with some sharing of parts. It was designed to create more of a "one-bedroom" liveaboard versus the "two-bedroom" layout on the Packet.

The accommodations are intended for use as a liveaboard for a couple, with occasional guests. The guests would berth either in the pilothouse or on the saloon settees. There is a washer and dryer plus tub and shower in the head. The galley has a full-size refrigerator-freezer, a 30" range with oven, and space for a small dish-washer, if desired. The desk would be a good place for a computer. The after deck could be screened or curtained for weather or bugs, and is often the nicest place for the dining table. It could be moved into the saloon in poor weather.

She has a ship-like Portuguese Bridge wrapping around the front of the pilothouse, giving a sheltered area for standing on deck, binoculars in place, scanning for the next mark or harbor entrance. There is plenty of boat deck space for carrying one or more small craft.

This 35-footer has many of the same features and livability found in our Friday Harbor Ferry series of designs. The difference is that this one has a pointed bow instead of the rounded bow of the ferries, which will let her go through a seaway without having to slow down quite as much. Construction could be done in either steel, fiberglass, or plywood and epoxy.

An alternative to the layout shown, for use with a family, would be to have berthing for the kids in the bow stateroom and making the berth and seat in the pilothouse into a double or queen-sized berth for the parents. However, this would take away a lot of the spacious, roomy feeling this open layout offers for full time life afloat.

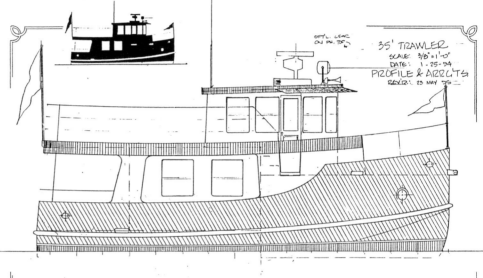

Particulars:

Length over guards		36'-0"
Length-structural		35'-4"
Designed waterline		34'-9"
Beam over guards		16'-0"
Beam-structural		15'-4"
Draft, loaded		3'-0"
Freeboard:	Forward	6'-7½"
	Waist	1'-11"
	Aft	1'-9"
Cruising Displ.*		40,400 lbs
Displ.-length ratio		409
Prismatic coefficient		.61
Pounds per inch imm.		2,140
Tankage:	Fuel	300 Gals.
	Water	500 Gals.
Stability - GM		6.7' to 4.4'

*CAUTION: The displacement quoted here is for the boat in cruising trim. That is, with the fuel and water tanks filled, the crew on board, as well as the crews' gear and stores in the lockers. This should not be confused with the "shipping weight" often quoted as "displacement" by some manufacturers. This should be taken into account when comparing figures and ratios between this and other designs.

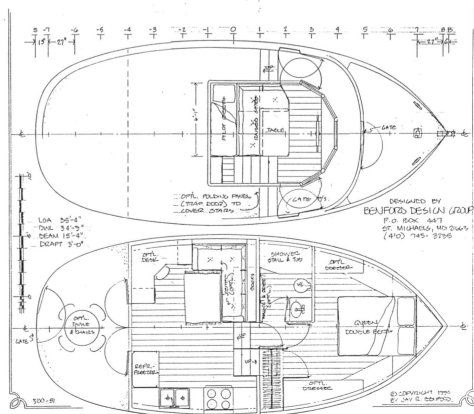

35' TRAWLER
SCALE: 3/8" = 1'-0"
DATE: 1-25-94
PROFILE & ARR'TS

LOA 35'-4"
DWL 34'-9"
BEAM 15'-4"
DRAFT 3'-0"

DESIGNED BY
BENFORD DESIGN GROUP
P.O. BOX 447
ST. MICHAELS, MD 21663
(410) 745-3235

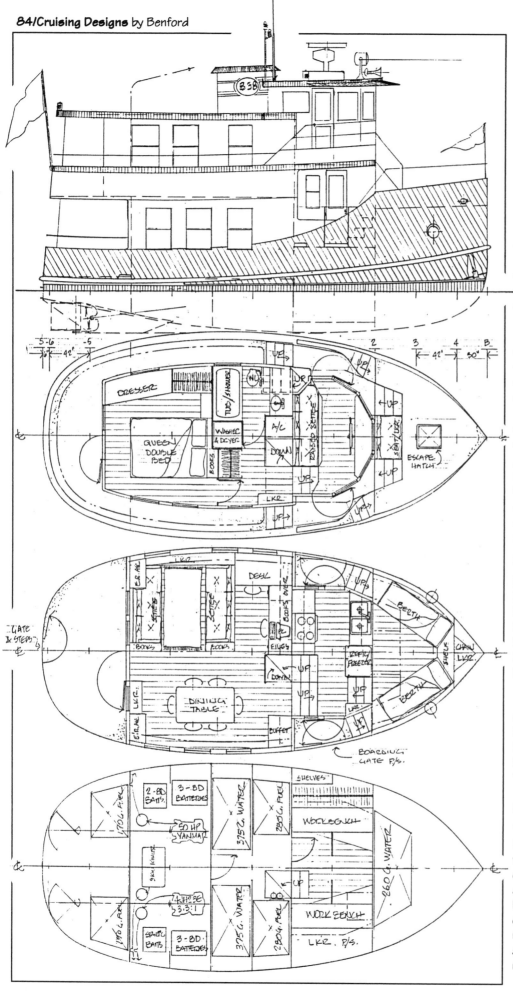

38' Packet

Design Number 334
1995

This design is another great liveaboard for a couple or a family. The accommodations have the master stateroom up and the guest stateroom in the bow. The head is up, adjoining the master, but with access from the passageway so it can be used by all the crew.

With two feet more beam than the 35' Packet, she can carry the raised saloon at the same level as the larger after deck. This also means the engine room can be under the saloon and the "basement" now can have a nice workshop.

The galley in the mid-level is close to both the pilothouse and the saloon. The saloon has a good-sized office in the forward port corner well suited to the tele-commuter.

Tankage is huge for a vessel of this size, permitting long periods away from shore-side facilities. With her great beam she has high stability needed for comfortable living aboard. While conceived as a coastwise cruiser, she could make Great Lakes crossings or transits to the Bahamas in reasonable weather.

Particulars:

Length over guards		38'-8"
Length-structural		38'-0"
Designed waterline		37'-6"
Beam over guards		18'-0"
Beam-structural		17'-4"
Draft, loaded		3'-6"
Freeboard:	Forward	7'-3"
	Waist	3'-9"
	Aft	1'-2"
Cruising Displ.*		60,000 lbs.
Displ.-length ratio		508
Prismatic coefficient		.585
Pounds per inch imm.		2,572
Tankage: Fuel		1,010 Gals.
Water		900 Gals.
Stability - GM		4' to 6.84'

*CAUTION: The displacement quoted here is for the boat in cruising trim. That is, with the fuel and water tanks filled, the crew on board, as well as the crews' gear and stores in the lockers. This should not be confused with the "shipping weight" often quoted as "displacement" by some manufacturers. This should be taken into account when comparing figures and ratios between this and other designs.

43' Freighter Yacht
Design Number 321
1992

This Freighter Yacht has an eight foot well deck, with room for a small (up to 2,000 lb.) vehicle to be carried on deck. By stacking the two berths on one side in the foc'sle, there's room for a complete head en suite.

The saloon has the living and dining room furniture. The mid-deck has a large galley plus an oilskin or coat closet.

The master stateroom is aft with an en suite full head. She has walkaround upper decks for that big ship feeling and practical ship handling.

The pilothouse has a good view over the skiff. The L-shaped settee is raised for visibility underway. The starboard aft corner is notched for the stairs to the boat deck.

The hold space shows an option for more berths if wanted, additional clothes lockers for out-of-season storage, and a fore and aft passageway from the foc'sle through the shop and laundry area to the saloon.

There is room for one or two small craft to be carried on top of the master stateroom, and a davit can be installed to lift them on and off.

The protective skegs under the rudders let the skipper feel there's no problem in going exploring in backwaters.

The rubber guard is the widest point of the boat, making for easy landings. This makes for a lot of peace of mind when making landings single-handed.

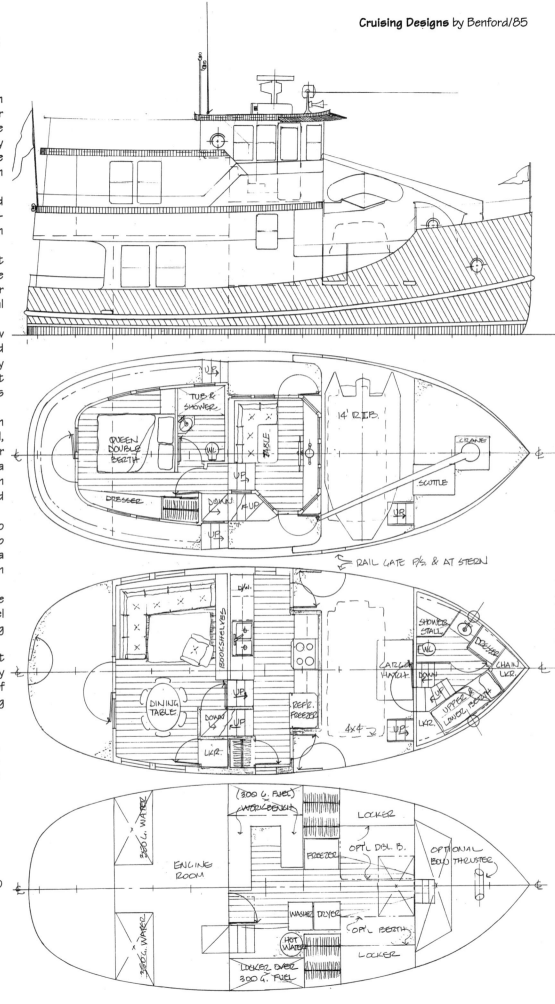

Particulars:	Wood	Steel
Length over guards	44'-0"	44'-0"
Length-structural	43'-4"	43'-4"
Designed waterline	42'-6"	42'-6"
Beam over guards	18'-0"	18'-0"
Beam-structural	17'-4"	17'-4"
Draft, loaded	4'-0"	4'-0"
Freeboard: Forward	7'-6"	7'-6"
Waist	4'-1"	4'-1"
Aft	1'-6"	1'-6"
Displacement, loaded for cruising	75,000	85,000
Displ.-length ratio	436	494
Pounds per inch imm.	3010	3010
Tankage, gals.: Fuel	500	600
Water	1,000	1,000
Stability - GM	4'	3.5'

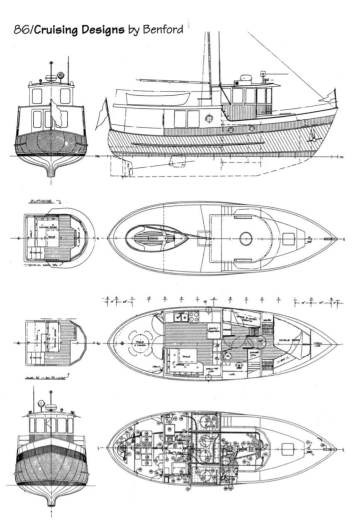

40', 56' & 64' TRAWLER YACHTS
Designs Number 324, 327 & 329
1992 & 1994

The 40' Trawler Yacht (left) is a available as from a molded fiberglass hull up to a completed boat from Cascade Yachts. She has a seakindly hull form and will have a comfortable motion underway.

She has two staterooms; the larger one forward as the owner's quarters and the smaller one under the pilothouse as the guest cabin. The head has a separate shower stall and good elbow room. There is plenty of room in the galley for people to get past the chef and/or bring in a couple chairs from the aft deck to sit around the saloon table in cooler or rainy weather. The after deck is generously sized and will be a popular place while aboard.

Her power requirements are modest, with a 50 hp diesel being the recommended powerplant. With enough reduction to swing a good sized prop this modest power will push her as fast as the hull form will permit.

Particulars:	40	56	64
Length overall	40'-0"	56'-0"	64'-0
Length designed waterline	34'-0"	53'-6"	61'-0"
Beam	12'-4"	20'-0"	20'-0"
Draft	3'-6"	5'-0"	5'-0"
Freeboard: Forward	8'-0"	8'-0"	8'-6"
Least	3'-4"	4'-0"	4'-0"
Aft	4'-4"	1'-9"	7'-6"
Displacement, cruising trim*, lbs.	21,750	135,000	145,500
Displacement-length ratio	247	394	286
Prismatic coefficient	.56	.55	.55
Water tankage, Gals.	300	1,250	1,260
Fuel tankage ,Gals.	315	1,800	2,550
Headroom	6'-1" to 6'-9"	6'-7"	6'-7"

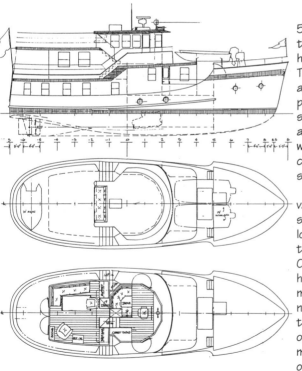

Both the 64' (left) and 56' (right) Trawlers have three staterooms and heads plus crew quarters. Their galley and dining area is under the pilothouse and their saloons are on the upper after deck. Their dumb waiters run up as the central column with the stairs winding around it.

These designs take advantage of the simplified structural design philosophy we evolved with the development of the Coasters. The hull forms have flared bows that are much finer than the original Coasters, being intended for more extended offshore work. This also makes them a bit easier on their power requirements for cruising speeds and will help stretch the fuel out on a long passage. This is just one of the many features that make these great cruising liveaboards.

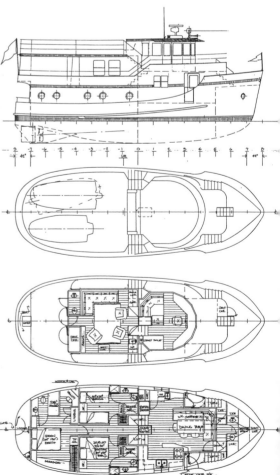

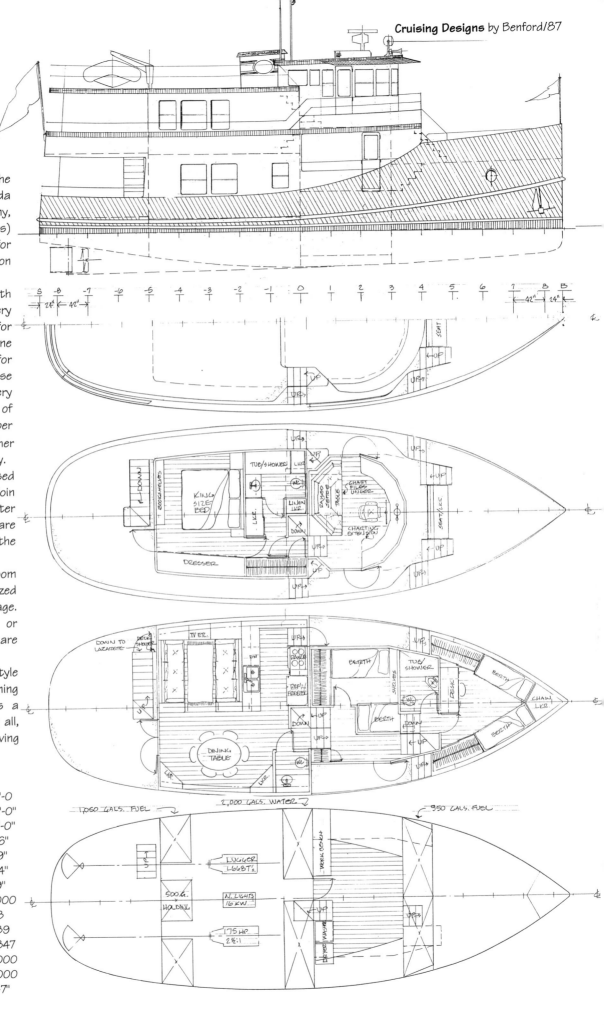

60' Motor Yacht

Design Number 337
1996

This design combines the best features of our Florida Bay Coaster designs (roomy, comfortable living quarters) with an easily driven hull for economy of operation on longer cruising.

We've added some length to this design to give very generous deck spaces for outdoor living. As anyone who has lived aboard for many years knows, these open deck spaces are very important and get a lot of use. The walk-around upper decks add greatly to her practicality & functionality.

The pilothouse has raised seating for the crew to join the helmsman. The after corners of the pilothouse are notched for stairs up to the boat deck.

The master stateroom has a full head, king-sized bed and generous storage. The forward two guest or children's staterooms share the head between them.

The family room style saloon, with galley and dining in it, is well proven as a practical solution. All in all, a great little ship for living aboard.

Particulars:

Length overall	60'-0
Length design waterline	60'-0"
Beam	20'-0"
Draft	4'-6"
Freeboard: Forward	7'-9"
Waist	4'-4"
Stern	1'-9"
Displ., cr'g. trim, lbs.	154,000
Displ.-length ratio	318
Prismatic coefficient	.589
Pounds per inch imm.	4,847
Tankage, gals.: water,	2,000
fuel	2,000
Headroom	6'-7"

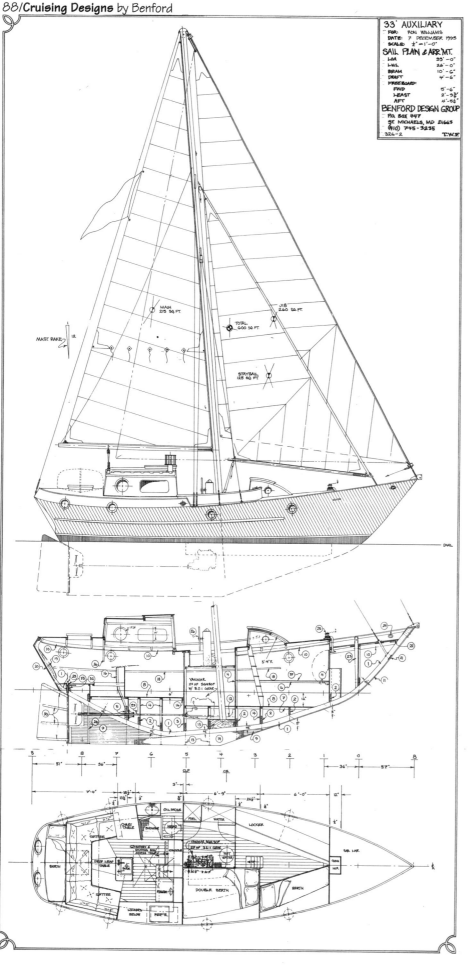

33' AUXILIARY
FOR: RON WILLIAMS
DATE: 7 DECEMBER 1993
SCALE: ½"=1'-0"
SAIL PLAN & ARR'MT.
 LOA   33'-0"
 LWL   26'-0"
 BEAM   10'-6"
 DRAFT   4'-6"
 FREEBOARD:
  FWD   5'-6"
  LEAST   2'-9¾"
  AFT   4'-5¼"

BENFORD DESIGN GROUP
P.O. BOX 447
ST. MICHAELS, MD 21663
(410) 745-3235
326-2   T.W.E.

33' Pilothouse Cutter

Design Number 326
1993

Often someone calls and says, "I like your design for this boat, but...."

That "but" often leads us off into the custom design territory. However, we can sometimes modify an existing design in a way that satisfies the needs of the clients and creates an interesting new boat in the process.

This design is just one of those instances. She carries the best features of **Bakea**'s Great Cabin layout from the the Benford 30 series. She also has an elegant spoon bow like **Antonia** plus the heart shaped transom and wineglass section hull form of the **Belle Amie** version. The net result is the creation of a shapely new classic sailing yacht.

Because of the way this design was done, by using parts of other designs to create a new one, her plan set combines sheets from other plan sets to be included with the stock plans. This lets us be creative in doing custom work by doing part of a new design and only charging for the partial custom design actually done.

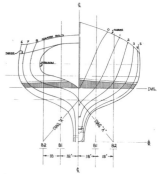

Particulars:		33	35
Length overall		33'-0"	35'-3"
Length design waterline		26'-0"	30'-4½"
Beam		10'-6"	10'-2¼"
Draft		4'-6"	4'-6"
Freeboard:	Forward	5'-6"	4'-3¾"
	Least	2'-9¾"	2'-2½"
	Aft	4'-5¼"	3'-1¼"
Displ., cruising trim, lbs.		13,265	19,000
Displacement-length ratio		337	303
Pounds per inch immersion		840	1,030
Ballast, lbs.		4,000	6,890
Ballast ratio		30%	36%
Sail area, Sq. Ft.		600	621
Sail area-displacement ratio		17.13	13.95
Prismatic coefficient		.54	.565
Entrance half-angle		24°	25°
Water tankage, Gals		88	160
Fuel tankage, Gals.		59	70
Headroom		6'-6"	6'-2"
GM		3.98'	2.8'

35' D.E. Schooner

Design Number 328
1994

This design originated from a request for a design like an older William Hand schooner he'd seen published. This presented an interesting challenge for us. We enlarged the small drawings that had been published and set about to try to recreate the shape in the computer. As often happens with small scale prints, they were distorted. We did the best we could to maintain the original character of the design while we created a shape that was fair both to the eye and to the computer. The result is a design that we now refer to as being "inspired by Bill Hand."

This computer work meant we could supply the builder with a set of computer faired and

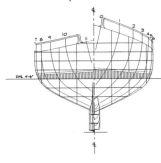

drawn full-size loftings to expedite the building process.

The design evolved in our office with the rough conceptuals being done with pencil on paper and the final drawings all done on a computer CAD program. We are doing more and more CAD drawings, with mixed feelings about it. It's not as fast as hand drawing originally, but if there are extensive revisions to be made the changes can be done very quickly. Also, if there is to be computer cutting of parts for the boat, doing the hull design in our Fast Ship program and the drawings on a CAD program greatly speeds up the process and makes for great accuracy of the final product.

(See the preceding page for her particulars.)

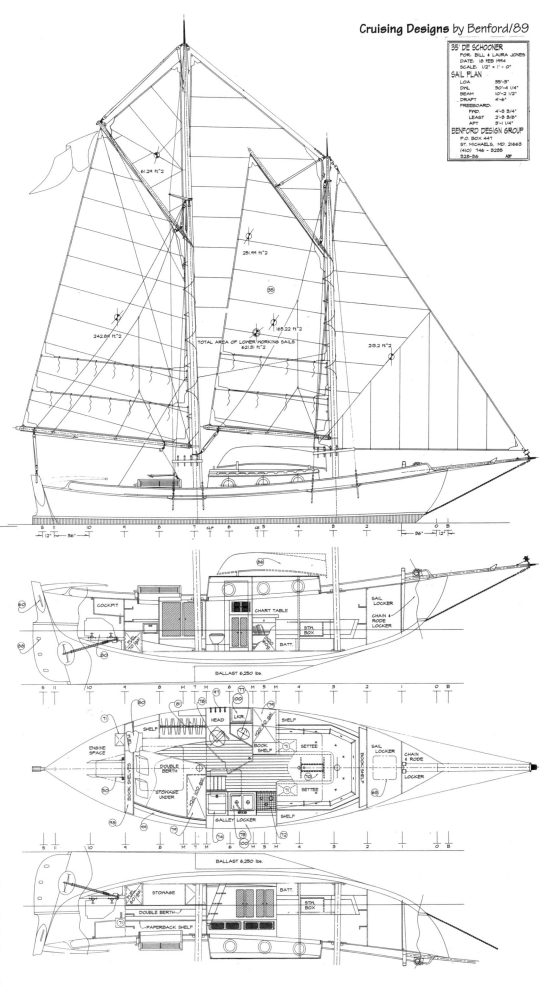

35' DE SCHOONER
FOR: BILL & LAURA JONES
DATE: 18 FEB 1994
SCALE: 1/2" = 1'-0"
SAIL PLAN
LOA   35'-3"
DWL   30'-4 1/4"
BEAM   10'-2 1/2"
DRAFT   4'-6"
FREEBOARD:
    FWD   4'-3 3/4"
    LEAST   2'-8 3/8"
    AFT   3'-1 1/4"
BENFORD DESIGN GROUP
P.O. BOX 447
ST. MICHAELS, MD. 21663
(410) 746 - 3235
328-36

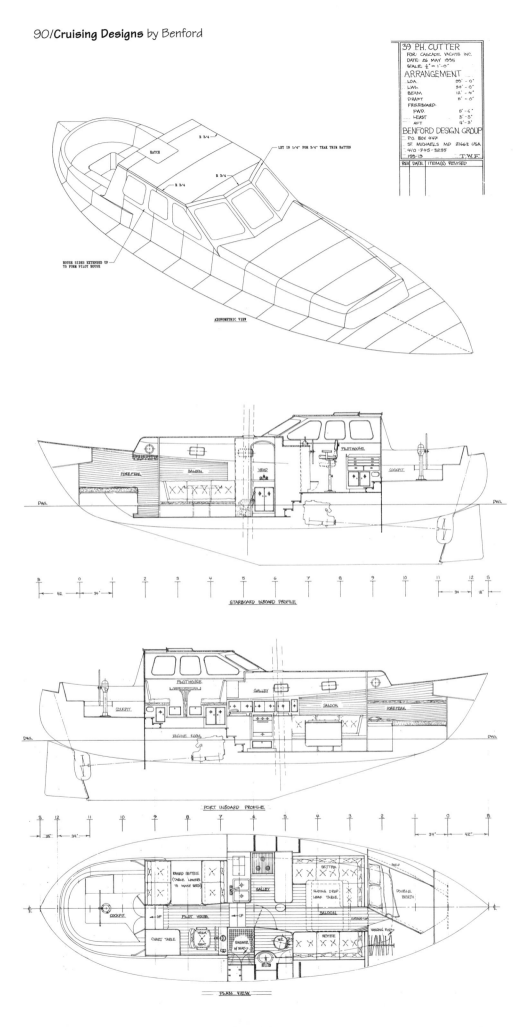

39 PH. CUTTER
FOR: CASCADE YACHTS INC.
DATE: 26 MAY 1995
SCALE: ¼" = 1'-0"

ARRANGEMENT
LOA . . . . 39'-0"
LWL . . . . 34'-0"
BEAM . . . . 12'-4"
DRAFT . . . . 5'-0"
FREEBOARD:
  FWD . . . . 5'-6"
  LEAST . . . . 3'-3"
  AFT . . . . 4'-3"

BENFORD DESIGN GROUP
P.O. BOX 447
ST. MICHAELS MD 21663 USA
410-745-3235
159-13   T.W.F.
REV DATE ITEM(S) REVISED

AXONOMETRIC VIEW

STARBOARD INBOARD PROFILE

PORT INBOARD PROFILE

PLAN VIEW

Cascade Classic 39 Pilothouse Cutter
Design Number 159
1977 & 1995

After producing many of the origin trunk cabin versions, the builders took one of the requests for a pilothou version. (See first version on p. 32 & 33.

The cockpit is virtually identical to th original 39'. It has high and well-slope seatbacks which are very comfortable fe long periods of time. The depth creates feeling of security of being "in" the boa rather than perched on it. There are hu storage spaces under the cockpit.

The pilothouse has a raised dinet which converts to a double berth. It elevated with good visibility, so the cre can see both where they're going an what's around them at anchor. The hel seat is at the inside steering station the starboard side of the pilothous Just aft of it is the one-fold chart tab (One-fold on standard sized charts.)

Under the pilothouse is the engi room, fuel tanks, pumps and batterie Hatches in the pilothouse sole give read access for checking the oil and servici the equipment. A couple more steps dow from the pilothouse is the galley to po and the head to starboard. The gall has good working areas and storage, bo under the counters and in overhe cabinets. The head has a separa shower stall. (The whole compartme won't have to be wiped dry after a showe Outboard of the shower seat is an oilsk locker, draining into the shower sump.

These offshore double enders are great size for a couple or a family to li and cruise aboard. They are of a size tha is roomy enough to carry long term stor and not be too crowded for daily living.

Particulars:		39PH	41
Length overall		39'-0	41'-0"
Length designed waterline		34'-0"	36'-0"
Beam		12'-4"	14'-0"
Draft		5'-0"	5'-0"
Freeboard:	Forward	5'-6"	6'-0"
	Least	3'-3"	3'-6"
	Aft	4'-3"	5'-11"
Displ., cruising trim, lbs.		23,275	27,67
Displacement-length ratio		264	265
Ballast, lbs.		8,000	8,30
Ballast ratio		34%	32%
Sail area, square feet		848	949
Sail area-displacement ratio		16.64	17.01
Prismatic coefficient		.557	.557
Pounds per inch immersion		1,367	1,552
Entrance half-angle		24¼°	22¼°
Tankage, gals.: water/ fuel		200/200	301/12
Headroom		6'-4" to 6'-8"	6'-10"

41' Great Cabin Cutter
Design Number 156
Revised 1992

The original version of this design, the 41' Cutter **Quiet Bird** is a very successful offshore double-ended cutter. When the request came along for this new design, to be based on one of our existing hulls, it made sense to us to use the beamy **Quiet Bird** hull to get all the room for this interior layout.

The midships cockpit has the seating at the after deck level, the coamings above deck and the footwell recessed into the deck. The windshield and canvas top will provide good shade and shelter for the on-watch crew.

The saloon is entered from the forward end of the cockpit . It has an L-shaped settee to starboard and a large dining table at the settee with a leaf that folds up for use by the chairs opposite. The forward port chair also serves the chart table.

Aft of the galley, in the great cabin, is the master stateroom. It has a queen sized berth with walk-around access on three sides. The shower stall has access from both the master and forward head. With the galley sink on the centerline counter adjacent to it, all the plumbing work is concentrated in this one area of the boat. Also, with the galley and head sinks near centerline, they won't back-flood on either tack.

The engine is located under the galley sink. Both the port and starboard sides of the enclosing box open up for accessing and servicing the engine.

The long keel is a foot shallower than the original fin keel. It's wineglass shape is built hollow with some tankage fitted into the keel. With some minor adjustments to the engine shaft angles, this keel could be used with the original **Quiet Bird** layout or the fin keel used with this one, if so desired. (For more information on the original **Quiet Bird**, see page 34.) (Preceding page has her particulars.)

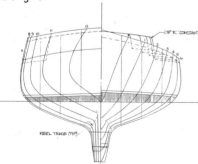

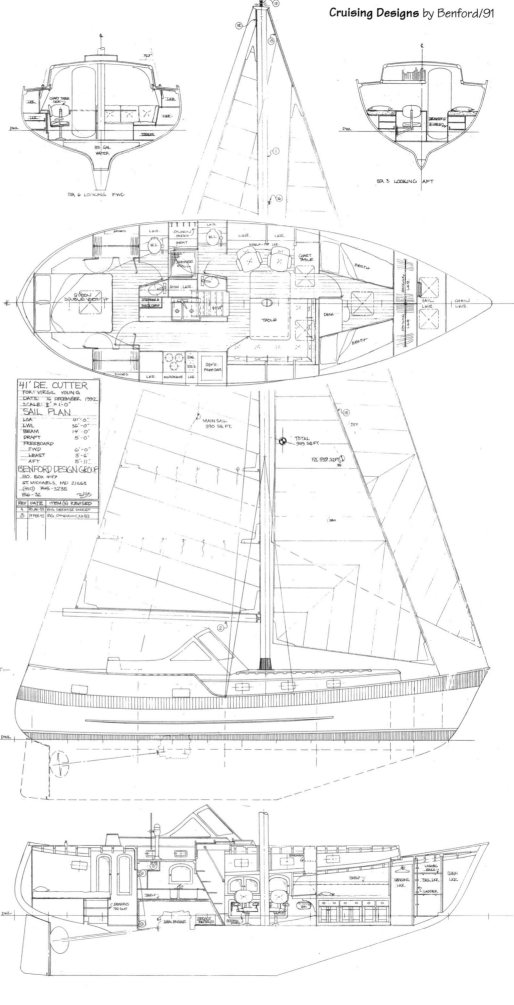

SAIL PLAN

41' D.E. CUTTER
FOR VIRGIL YOUNG
DATE: 16 DECEMBER 1992
SCALE: ¼" = 1'-0"

LOA	41'-0"
LWL	36'-0"
BEAM	14'-0"
DRAFT	5'-0"
FREEBOARD	
FWD	6'-0"
LEAST	3'-6"
AFT	5'-11"

BENFORD DESIGN GROUP
P.O. BOX 447
ST. MICHAELS, MD 21663
(410) 745-3235
156-32

REV	DATE	ITEM(S) REVISED
A	30 JAN 93	ENG DECREASE RUDDER
B	17 FEB 93	BG. DIMENSIONS, NOTES

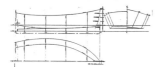

7-3" Dinghy
7'-3" x 6'-9" x 3'-9¼" x 0'-4"

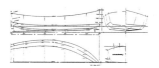

7½' Dinghy
7'-6" x 7 x 3'-9" x 0'-5"

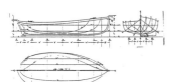

8' Double-Ended Dinghy
8' x 7'-3¾" x 3' x 0'-4"

8' Portland Yawlboat
8' x 7'-6" x 4' x 0'-5"/2'-6"

8½' Dinghy
8'-6" x 8'-2½" x 4' x 0'-9"/2'-6"

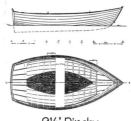

9½' Dinghy
9'-6" x 8'-3" x 4'-6" x 0'-7"

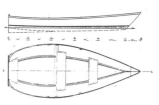

11'-4" Dinghy
11'-4" x 10'-1" x 4'-6" x 0'-3"

9' Pacific Peapod
9' x 8'-6" x 4'-6" x 0'-7"/2'-9"

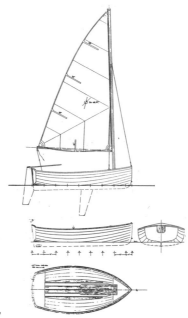

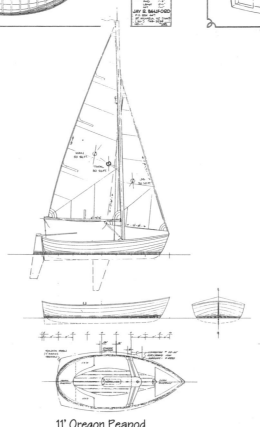

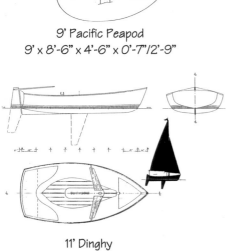

11' Dinghy
11' x 10' x 5' x 0'-6"/3'

11' Oregon Peapod
11' x 10' x 4'-6" x 0'-6"/3'

11' Dinghy **Night**
11' x 9'-6" x 4' 0'-6"/2'-11"

SMALL CRAFT PLANS

"Let's get it straight up front: This book is more than a catalog of designs. The 96 pages between its covers contain plans for 15 small craft. Designer Jay Benford knows that readers will build directly from the book — bypassing the formality of ordering plans from his office.   In fact he encourages the process by including full working drawings and tables of offsets for all of the designs."   **WoodenBoat**

The 15 sets of complete plans for skiffs & tenders from the Boards of the Benford Design Group (as shown on these two pages) will help you build your own dinghy, small craft, or tender. Plans for 7'-3" to 18-footers in cold-molded, carvel, lapstrake, plywood, and fiberglass construction are included, along with photos of some completed boats. 96 pages, softcover.

To order this book of plans with your Visa or Mastercard, call our toll-free order line:

1-800- 6TILLER.

For a brochure with prices for plans and books, write to us at:

P. O. Box 447
St. Michaels, MD 21663

12' Keelboat
12' x 12' x 5' x 3'-4½"

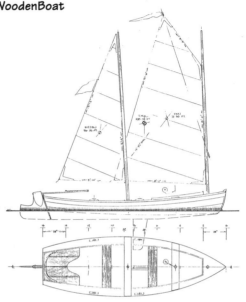

16' *Conch Ad Libitum*
16' x 15' x 5' x 0'-9"/3'-3"

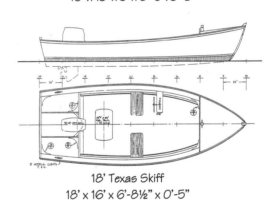

18' Texas Skiff
18' x 16' x 6'-8½" x 0'-5"

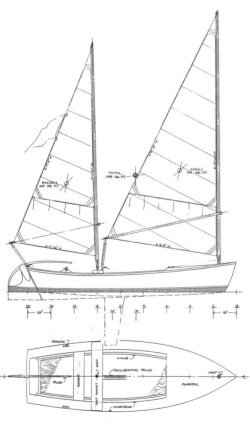

18' Cat Ketch
18' x 16' x 6' x 0'-8"/4'-6"

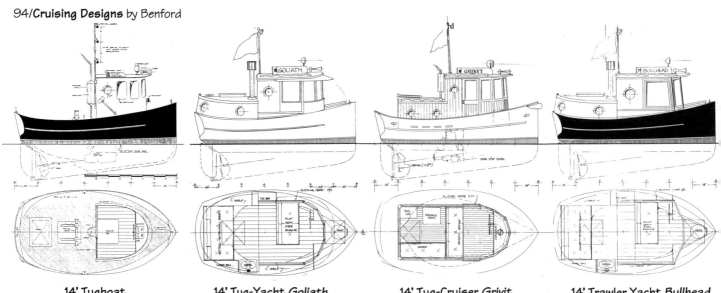

14' Tugboat
14' x 13' 7" x 3'

14' Tug-Yacht Goliath
14' x 13' 7" x 3'

14' Tug-Cruiser Grivit
14' x 13' 7" x 3'

14' Trawler Yacht Bullhead
14' x 13' 7" x 3'

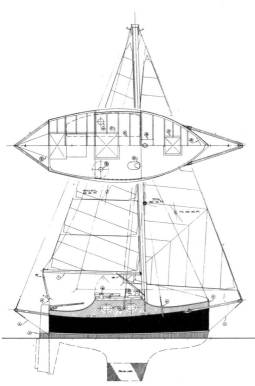

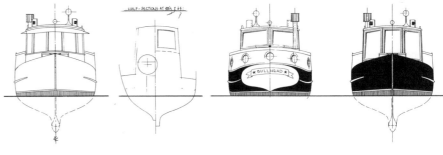

POCKET CRUISERS & TABLOID YACHTS
— VOLUME 1 —

Complete building plans for the small cruising boats shown on these two pages are in our book, POCKET CRUISERS & TABLOID YACHTS, VOLUME 1. These boats are some of the most popular plans from the boards of the Benford Design Group. They're shown in full detail in this 96 page, 8½" x 11" softcover book.

"All of the plans exhibit the professional presentation and well-conceived accommodations typical of the author's work."

WoodenBoat

14' Cruiser Happy
13'-10" x 18'-8" x 6'-3" x 3'-7"

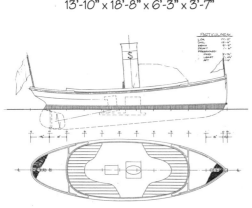

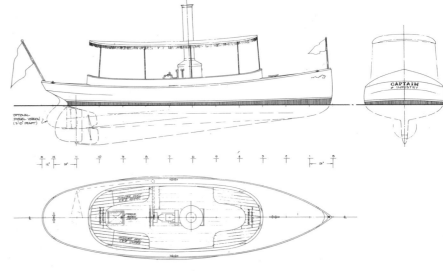

17' Fantail Steam Launch Myf
17 x 15'-6" x 5'-3" x 1'-8"

25' Fantail Steam Launch Beverley
25' x 22'-6" x 7' x 3'-3"

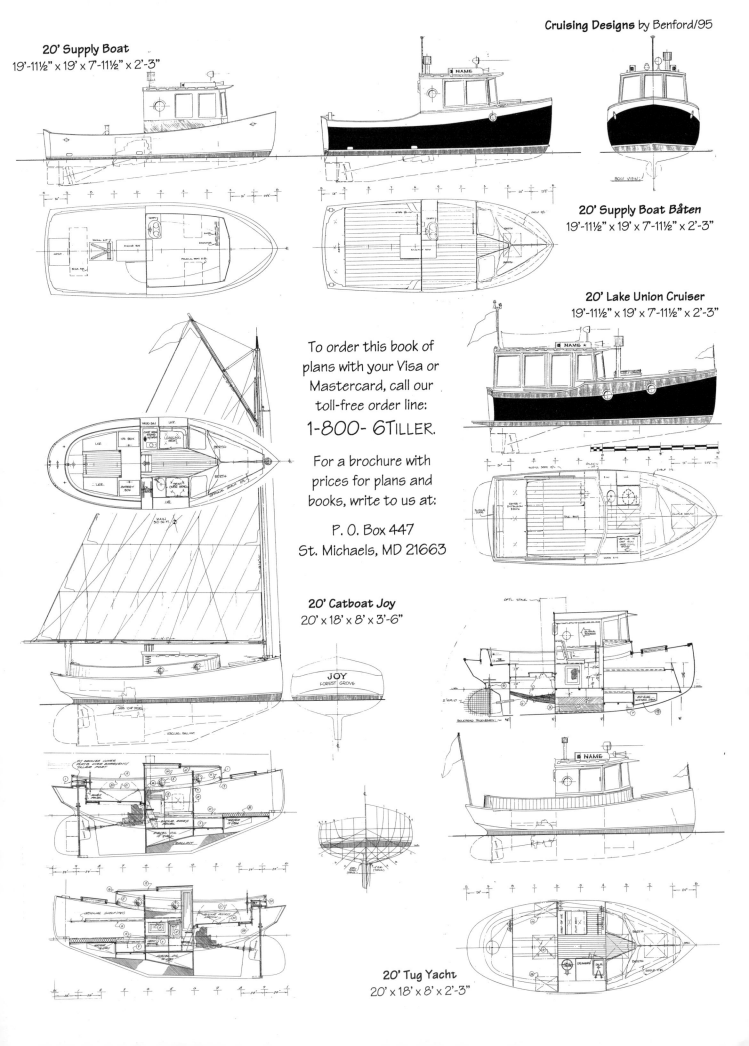

20' Supply Boat
19'-11½" x 19' x 7'-11½" x 2'-3"

20' Supply Boat Båten
19'-11½" x 19' x 7'-11½" x 2'-3"

20' Lake Union Cruiser
19'-11½" x 19' x 7'-11½" x 2'-3"

To order this book of plans with your Visa or Mastercard, call our toll-free order line:

1-800- 6TILLER.

For a brochure with prices for plans and books, write to us at:

P. O. Box 447
St. Michaels, MD 21663

20' Catboat Joy
20' x 18' x 8' x 3'-6"

JOY
FOREST GROVE

20' Tug Yacht
20' x 18' x 8' x 2'-3"

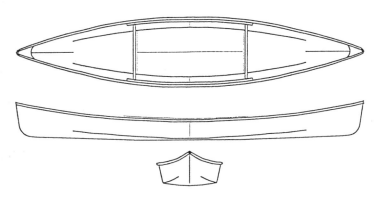

BUILDING SWEET DREAM

An ultralight solo canoe for single and double paddle. This book is a complete how-to manual covering all phases of building and finishing. It includes dimensioned hull plans, detailed building sequence, tips and techniques for painting and varnishing, and hard-to-find background and reference material.

Sweet Dream is easily and quickly built using hand and basic electric tools.

Sweet Dream can be easily built by one person in a one-car garage or small workshop. Using the "folded ply" techniques shown in this book, you can build 12', 13', or 14' canoes. Marc Pettingill shows how 2 sheets of 4mm okume ply (plus some epoxy & trim) produce a 27-lb. rounded hull canoe. 8½" x 11", softcover, 192 pages. –

BUILDING THE SIX-HOUR CANOE

Quickly and simply built, the Six-Hour Canoe is suitable for builders and paddlers young and old — a wonderful way to get afloat. 8½"x11", 65 pages, Softcover, many photos & drawings.

PRACTICAL JUNK RIG

Hasler & McLeod wrote this definitive handbook for designing, building and sailing junk rigged vessels. Reading it will show you why short-handed sailors love this rig.

Hardcover, 8½"x11", 244 pages, drawings, tables, photos & how-to design your own junk rig information. "There is no better or more comprehensive work on the subject available...it should be considered THE handbook on junk rigs for anyone interested in the subject." **Sailing**

Marchaj's SEAWORTHINESS
THE FORGOTTEN FACTOR

Newly updated & revised, this book is a highly readable survey of the seaworthiness of modern yacht designs. Based on the highest degree of practical and academic research, it shows how modern yachts often sacrifice safety for speed and other considerations, and explains how ideas about design still need to be changed to prevent loss of life. Hardcover, 7¾"x10½", 384 pages with 140 line drawings & 50 photos. "For the first time we are offered logical scientific criteria which help us to assess the likely seaworthiness of one boat or another. **Practical Boat Owner**

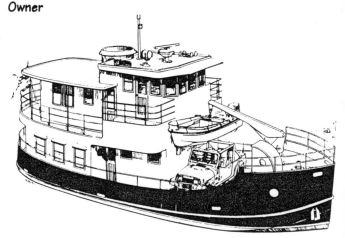

SMALL SHIPS, THIRD EDITION

Study plans from the Benford Design Group for tugs, freighters, ferries, excursion boats, trawler yachts, houseboats & fishing vessels, 8½"x11", softcover, 304 pages. "I have spent **hours** perusing SMALL SHIPS to my utter delight. Here is Benford at his best....original, fun, and thought provoking." **Coastal Cruising**

STEEL BOATBUILDING

by Thomas E. Colvin; from plans to bare hull & bare hull to launching. 7" x 10" 480 pages softcover with many illustrations. "There is probably no one more uniquely qualified to pen the ultimate book on steel boatbuilding than author, designer, builder and live-aboard cruising man Tom Colvin." **Cruising World**